EBURY PRESS
RHYTHMIC PARENTING

Aprajita D. Sadhu co-founded Ukti, the first Waldorf school in North India, as a passion project. With her vision and guidance, Ukti grew into a place where teachers taught from inspiration and children learnt with joy and vigour. Inspired by the work, she left her career as an economist to teach middle-schoolers through the Covid-19 pandemic—a powerful and transformative experience. Today, she teaches high-schoolers at the San Francisco Waldorf School and enjoys learning from the younger generation. Her conviction in the human potential to create a life of purpose drives her to grow new capacities in herself and inspire others to do the same.

Salone Zutshi is an educator whose work has been enriched by her background as a sociologist. What began as a pursuit of meaningful education for her children, culminated in her co-founding Ukti, the first Waldorf school in North India. With hands-on work teaching children, training teachers, developing curricula and guiding parents, Salone grew the school from the grassroots to a thriving learning community, creating long-term positive impact in many lives. Today, she educates parents on raising children in developmentally appropriate ways.

ADVANCE PRAISE FOR THE BOOK

'As a paediatrician and adolescent doctor, I know the many negative effects of educational practices that are not oriented towards the developmental needs of children and adolescents, including screen consumption, which happens much too early and runs counter to healthy sensorimotor development, which can only take place in the analog world. I hope this book achieves a wide distribution so that parents and guardians put themselves at the service of the next generation and create conditions that enable healthy development in the digital age'—**Michaela Glöckler, MD, former head, Medical Section, Goetheanum, Switzerland**

'This book is a unique and creative approach to parenting. It celebrates a child's agency and consciousness, beautifully describing how children naturally think, feel, live, experience and make sense of the world. The approach foregrounds the joys of natural childhood over predetermined notions of how children should be. This is compellingly applied to the full spectrum of issues: health, nutrition, sleep, play, literacy, learning, and social and emotional development. A must-read for all'—**Namita Ranganathan, former head and dean, Department of Education, Delhi University**

'Through rhythm, a child gains integrated experience as a physical, emotional and intellectual being to develop a true sense of self. Parents will find in this book an empathetic ear to their everyday concerns and frustrations. The thoughtful and intentional advice will empower them to embrace their child's unique developmental journey with reverence and grace'—**Nikhil Rishi Mehra, founder/chief design officer, Shantnu & Nikhil, and former parent at Ukti Waldorf**

Rhythmic Parenting

WHAT YOUR CHILD NEEDS TO THRIVE IN A FAST-MOVING WORLD

APRAJITA D. SADHU
SALONE ZUTSHI

EBURY PRESS

An imprint of Penguin Random House

EBURY PRESS

Ebury Press is an imprint of the Penguin Random House group of companies whose addresses can be found at global.penguinrandomhouse.com

Published by Penguin Random House India Pvt. Ltd
4th Floor, Capital Tower 1, MG Road,
Gurugram 122 002, Haryana, India

First published in Ebury Press by Penguin Random House India 2025

Copyright © Aprajita D. Sadhu and Salone Zutshi 2025

All rights reserved

10 9 8 7 6 5 4 3 2 1

The views and opinions expressed in this book are the authors' own and the facts are as reported by them which have been verified to the extent possible, and the publishers are not in any way liable for the same.

Please note that no part of this book may be used or reproduced in any manner for the purpose of training artificial intelligence technologies or systems.

ISBN 9780143473725

Typeset in Adobe Caslon Pro by MAP Systems, Bengaluru, India

This book is sold subject to the condition that it shall not, by way of trade or otherwise, be lent, resold, hired out or otherwise circulated without the publisher's prior consent in any form of binding or cover other than that in which it is published and without a similar condition including this condition being imposed on the subsequent purchaser.

www.penguin.co.in

*We dedicate this book to our parents, Kiran and Ajit Zutshi,
who gave us the gifts of questioning, seeking and
lifelong striving*

This book would not have been possible without
the understanding and support of our family,
the constant prodding by our friends and their belief in
our work, and the lifelong learning relationships with
the children, parents, colleagues and mentors of the
worldwide Waldorf community.

Contents

Why This Book xi

1. Consciousness and Task of a Young Child 1
2. Rhythm: A Cradle for Healthy Growth 18
3. Screen Time: An Intense Inbreath 48
4. The Place of Education in the Rhythm of Growth 72
5. Social Engagements: An Avoidable Inbreath 121
6. How Parents Impact the Rhythm of Growth 135
7. Eating: The Most Important Inbreath 155
8. Play: When Children Naturally Harmonize Inbreath and Outbreath 175
9. Home Chores: A Highly Effective Outbreath 205
10. Sleep: The Deepest Outbreath 219

Recommended Reading 237

Why This Book

Today, young children are growing up in a world that values speed and efficiency above all else. This world fails to provide the right conditions for children's primary task in the first seven years—physical development. Instead, its hyper-productive, hi-tech culture pushes children into becoming little adults—prematurely intellectualized and ill-adjusted in their bodies. Forced to grow up too soon, they skip important developmental steps along the way. When children are not allowed to be children, they struggle to become adults.

Rhythmic Parenting presents a comprehensive picture of the child during the early years and explains how the current milieu crowds out the child's true needs, warping their course of development. The book empowers parents to reclaim their child's place in our fast-moving world by taking the following steps:

- **Understand** that a young child has a vastly different consciousness compared to an adult. In the first seven years of life, the child has a sponge-like impressionability. The world flows into them unhindered and they imbibe it with a loving openness. Psychologists have found evidence that 'children notice what adults tend to miss . . . (because they can) distribute attention across multiple dimensions'.[1] By constantly soaking up impressions from their surroundings (inbreaths) and digesting them (outbreaths), the child wakes up to the physical world and forms their physical self. This learning and development are early childhood education.

- **Recognize** that children are growing up in a world that is constantly generating intense impressions. The ubiquity of screens and content, the pressures of academic learning and the culture of being treated like adults create powerful inbreaths that children cannot help but absorb. However, they

---

[1] D.J. Plebanek and V.M. Sloutsky, 'Costs of Selective Attention: When Children Notice What Adults Miss', *Psychol. Sci.* 2017 June 28(6):723–32.

struggle to digest them. Then there is the morning rush to get to school, a heated conversation between adults, getting stuck in traffic, and the child has a sort of sensory bloating by the end of the day. The result is malaise—children stuck with undigested impressions that parents experience as difficult behaviours.

- **Curate** a healthy rhythm for your child by minimizing intense inbreaths and balancing them with expansive outbreaths. The book offers step-by-step guidance to limiting intense inbreaths, from weaning your child off the screen and choosing a healthy preschool for them to socializing them in a developmentally appropriate manner and bringing awareness to your interactions with them so you neither infantilize them nor treat them as an adult. The rest of the book encourages parents to prioritize outbreaths in the child's rhythm. Nature-based experiences such as running barefoot on grass, digging in the sandpit and rolling down a hill are especially important for children whose daily environment exposes them to intense impressions. Daily play time needs to be protected so that the child can be free to work out undigested inbreaths. Daily chores such as washing dishes, mopping the floor and cutting vegetables are especially effective outbreaths. And finally, maintaining consistent nap times and bedtime is the ultimate solution for balancing inbreaths.

Our advice comes from many years of daily, challenging and extremely rewarding hands-on work with children at Ukti, the first Waldorf school we co-founded in North India, and in Waldorf schools around the San Francisco Bay Area. *Rhythmic Parenting* distils our experience across two continents with vastly different cultures, which reaffirmed one truth every time: that for every child, rhythm creates health. Whether it was a child who could not sit still for a minute, a child who could not run, a child who avoided eye contact, a child who barely spoke, a child who talked all the time and could not participate in activities, a child who routinely disrupted other children's play, a child who couldn't bear a drop of water touching them, a child who ate nothing all day or a child who couldn't fall asleep at night, in every case, by bringing stimulation in balance with rest, the child began to heal and thrive.

Rhythmic Parenting is a must-read for parents who are raising children without a 'village' and constantly sifting through piecemeal solutions. While the book addresses parents as the primary advocates of their child's well-being, its timely and practical guidance will appeal to educators, stakeholders and policymakers alike.

Chapter 1

Consciousness and Task of a Young Child

You are the parent of a young child. There is a lot to do. You need to feed them, bathe them, take them to the park and more. There is a similar list for tomorrow and a more elaborate plan for the weekend. As you check off one box after another, handling your child as best as you can, you have questions about what you're doing and whether you're doing it right. The to-do list keeps growing with the child, and so do the questions. It can be difficult to figure out where to begin. The answer is simple. Begin with the child.

Who Is the Young Child?

Imagine feeling like you were the whole universe. Like the sun shone inside you, the birds sang in your heart and the light of distant stars filled your mind. When the oceans swelled, you felt powerful. When the trees swayed, you danced with them. You belonged to the mountains, streams and meadows. You felt an affection for everything, near and far, from the ant crawling beside you to the people on the street. Like you were in love. And the world loved you and held you in its arms.

This is a young child and how they relate to the world. Everything flows into them, and they resist nothing. Their consciousness stretches far beyond the little bodies they have just arrived in. You can see a glimpse of this expansiveness in a baby's eyes. Their gaze belongs everywhere and beholds everything. It is a kind of spiritual oneness that fills them with a deep trust in the world. The world is good. A fly may happily sit on a baby's arm, and they will not be bothered by it, unlike an adult, who will shoo it away immediately. The fly feels like an extension of themselves, just like everything else in their surroundings. The child and the world are one. A seamless whole.

Bit by bit, with every little interaction, they wake up to the physical reality around them, starting with their own body. When they drink milk, it spills out of their mouth. When they burp, they drool. The adult steps in to wipe them. When the cloth brushes against their skin, they gain a momentary awareness of their body. When a nursing baby pulls at their mother's earring, they're discovering the object they just touched and how their body is different from it, gaining a sense of both. When they start eating solid foods, they happily paint themselves with it. This is their way of getting to know the food and, through its texture, their skin. Here's Bernard Lievegoed, a Dutch doctor and psychiatrist, describing a child's first 'toys'.

> . . . the child's own body is also an unknown part of the outside world. Hands, waving through the field of vision, are discovered and used as the first toy. Then the legs are discovered and grasped, only to disappear suddenly, nowhere to be found. This is the same comic performance as that of a young kitten trying to catch its own tail. Once the baby has discovered his own body in that part of the world which is his, he can gradually use it to discover other parts of the world.[1]

---

[1] C.J. Bernard Lievegoed, *Phases of Childhood: Growing in Body, Soul and Spirit*. Edinburgh, UK: Floris Books, 2005.

The young child's open stance makes them interested in everything around them. They are eager to touch everything and are filled with awe at each discovery. These interactions are the foundation of learning about the world and, through it, about their own physicality. It is the ground on which the child, over the years, transitions from a state of oneness to feeling separated from the world. This is a long process of incarnation—of inhabiting the body and becoming a person of the world. In the first seven years of life, this process takes place through bodily experiences.

As a baby, even when they are just lying on their backs, they are absorbing impressions from their environment: sounds, smells, sights and more. They are doing a lot of work, which is not always obvious to the adult eye: drinking milk and eliminating, sleeping and waking, taking in myriad impressions from their environment and processing them. Every now and then, when they are picked up and carried around, they get a peek into the whole wide world that awaits them and are momentarily catapulted to a future capability. This can be quite exciting, and, at times, overwhelming for them. Before too long, the next milestone happens. When they can turn their neck and, soon after, roll over, a new world of possibilities opens up. Now, they can turn and find you when they hear your voice and grab their favourite toy by rolling over.

When babies begin to crawl, a second dimension of learning opens. They move constantly to explore this new world. You look away for a second and they have crawled to the end of the hallway. Every time they bump into a wall or a table, it awakens them just a little bit more to where their body ends and where the world begins. Like a bee in a spring garden, flitting from flower to flower, they are drawn to the next thing that catches their fancy. The mop is as interesting as a strawberry. Everything needs to be touched, held, put in their tiny mouths, dirt and fruit alike, until something tells them after repeated experiences that fruit is better than dirt. When they meticulously empty kitchen drawers and take out the spoons and bowls one by one and put them back, only to take them out again and repeat the whole process several times, an adult might find it purposeless or boring (even annoying). But, for a child, doing it repeatedly helps them learn about the spoons, the bowls and the drawer. The young child doesn't know the concepts of material, weight or size, but through repetition, they gain a bodily understanding of these qualities. This is learning by doing—the only way young children learn.

As they continue to grow at this stage, they become eager to rise up. They cannot wait to see more. If they have an older sibling, you might find them gaping at the sight of their sibling walking with ease. They push themselves to stand, taking the support of whatever is available—a table, a chair, a human—then topple over and try again. One day they achieve this remarkable feat after persistent effort. Now as they begin to cruise, they fall from time to time. Every time this happens, they gain the knowledge that grass is different from concrete, which is different from a wooden floor. More and more of the world flows into them.

When they begin to walk, they take their first firm step towards becoming a human being. Who is to stop them from embracing the world, now that they are not horizontal any more? They can get to everything, everywhere, faster, whether in the living room or in the middle of a crowded mall. They can reach new heights, literally. And, with their hands now freed from crawling, they can do much more.

The world is their playground and the possibilities are endless. Now, exploration and play advance to the next stage.

Not only can they touch, pick and drop things, now they can carry them around. When they stack wooden blocks on top of one another and walk across the room to bring back a toy plane to place on top of the stack, they are delighted by their new creation. When they dig their hands in the sand and make a castle, gather some twigs to plant in the garden of their castle, and fill water in a can to water the 'trees', they are not only using what's around them but transforming it. The child is learning that when they follow their interest, explore their surroundings and create something that didn't exist before, they can change the world.

Learning of the world goes hand in hand with learning about themselves. When they happily pour water on themselves while watering a plant, they become aware of their body feeling wet; they could not have known this any other way, especially not from an advance warning from you. When they run over to you and want to dip their cookie in your tea, you try to warn them that it's hot. But that means nothing to them. It is only when they touch the cup and feel the heat that they understand. The next time you give them soup, they will touch it and tell you that it's hot.

Soon, you might find them picking up a spoon and walking around the house talking on the 'phone', beating 'eggs' in an empty bowl to make you an 'omelette', or putting their doll to sleep by gently rocking it. They might repeat phrases they've heard from Grandma or hum music from the radio. As they become more capable in their bodies and speech, they imitate impressions from their environment.

This everyday picture of the child in the first seven years looks playful and frivolous. What are they up to with all this busy work?

The Child's Task in the First Seven Years

The picture of the young child shared above is one of constantly exploring, interacting with, separating from and developing out of the physical reality around them. Throughout this process, the child is learning about this reality so they can inhabit more and more of it. This is their twin task of growth and learning.

The most visible sign of growth is the sheer amount of physical development the young child undertakes in the first seven years. From cuddly legs that are just a bit longer than the head in the first year, the child grows rhythmically, stretching in limbs, then in breadth, back and forth, until by five, the adorable thigh folds disappear, and muscles and joints begin to form. The torso lengthens, the neck emerges and the chin comes forward to convey facial expressions. From this point on, the limbs continue to grow and become slender, and the torso becomes slimmer with an S-shaped spinal curvature, and around the age of seven, the head is a sixth of the body. This growth is the main task of the child. Unlike a baby in the womb that receives all that is needed for growth, the young child during the first seven years grows through their active interaction with their environment.

This outward growth that is visible to parents and is carefully tracked by paediatricians has an inner counterpart that is less obvious and typically receives less attention. These are the four senses of life, touch, movement and balance that children develop during the early years as a foundation for healthy physical, emotional and intellectual development throughout life.

Sense of Life

The sense of life kicks in soon after birth and continues to develop during the early years. It is this sense that tells us that our body is healthy, leading to a feeling of comfort and well-being. It tells us when we are tired or sleepy, hungry or have eaten too much, cold or warm, or when we are ill. This sense is easiest to notice when it is disturbed, for example, when we sleep late at night, wake up groggy the next morning and feel a bit off. Similarly, before we come down with a fever, something doesn't feel right, but we cannot put a finger on it. When we are injured, the pain we feel is the disturbance in this sense of life. The sense of life warns us when we are not in a state of harmony and wellness. Pain and discomfort make us pay attention to our body and take action. Here is Bernard Lievegoed again, painting a beautiful picture of this sense as it starts to develop in a baby:

> When the warm, sweet milk flows into (a baby's) body . . . the whole body, including the little kicking feet and tiny grasping hands, is involved in the tasting. When the baby has drunk his fill . . . he sinks into a satisfied state of unconsciousness until the feeling of hunger again conjures up a reaction of dissatisfaction . . . He screams and kicks, waving his arms and throwing his body around, until it is covered in sweat and completely

exhausted. When he is breastfed again, after being changed, he will greedily suck the milk . . . A quiet glow spreads over the whole body.[2]

With every feeding of nutritious food, massaging their back to help them burp, changing their diaper so they are clean and dry, putting on a layer to keep them warm, and rocking them to sleep, the baby develops a sense of bodily well-being. When such care is missed or delayed, they cry and are quick to let us know. This is a healthy sign.

Fulfilling these vital needs continues to be crucial throughout early childhood for developing the life sense. This is why it is so important that even as children grow to be three, five and seven years old, they are reminded to wear layers when it gets cold or put on socks when their feet are frosty. When one or more of these needs are routinely neglected, the sense of life does not develop properly. Such children do not feel at ease in their bodies. They feel unsafe, insecure and can easily become anxious. They struggle to play by themselves or with other children. Because the

---

[2] Bernard C.J. Lievegoed, *Phases of Childhood: Growing in Body, Soul and Spirit*. Edinburgh, UK: Floris Books, 2005, pp. 54–55.

body is the vehicle with which the child reaches into the world, takes in the world and makes it a part of themselves, both learning and development are compromised when the child does not feel comfortable in their body.

Sense of Touch

Touch is the first sense to be awakened. During labour, as the walls of the womb surge and recede, the baby moves to the birth canal and continues to be moved along by expansion and contraction. During this time, they experience pressure and release, sensing their body for the first time. However, this is only a sleeping consciousness. Over the next several years, the child will have myriad interactions with their environment that will develop their sense of touch.

A child who is given the freedom to explore their surroundings in diverse ways—from climbing trees and grasping the coarseness of tree bark, from soft leaves brushing against their skin to being covered in mud from head to toe, from feeling the moist grass beneath their feet to stepping on a pebble—is waking up to the world through touch.

Sometimes, children can be oversensitive to touch. They avoid getting wet, running barefoot on grass, touching certain foods or wearing fitted clothing or socks with seams. They might feel overly constricted when hugged, feeling it as an assault on their body.

Since touch is the primary sense through which a child becomes aware of where their body ends and where the world begins, the young child actively learns about the world through touch. In this sense, touch is foundational for education, and it is important to develop it in the early years. Baby carrying, skin-to-skin contact, massages and swaddling, all help develop a healthy sense of touch in the infant and toddler. As they get older, young children benefit from regular bear hugs and games where they are wrapped in a rug, rolled back and forth as if they were dough, and patted into pancakes.

When the sense of touch is cultivated well in early childhood, the child goes on to develop a clear and strong sense of who they are. They stand in a healthy relationship to the world; they do not trespass into someone else's space and, at the same time, do not allow others to walk over them. When standing in a queue, such children will maintain their distance, and neither push against others nor be okay with getting pushed. When the child has not had enough touch experiences in their early years, their sense of self remains weak. They will find it difficult to say 'no' to experiences that are uncomfortable and might say 'yes' just to please others.

Twin Senses of Movement and Balance

As the child learns to stand and walk, two senses help a child feel at home in their physical body: a spatial awareness of where they are in relation to their surroundings (sense of movement) and how stable and secure they feel (sense of balance). We are not born with these senses, which is evident from watching a toddler move around. We develop these senses in the early years through various kinds of movement. Every time a child moves their arms and legs, they get to know their physical body a little bit. A child who gets to hop, skip, somersault, slide, swing and climb a hill, starts to feel more and more at home in their body. By making space and time for the child to follow their natural urge to move and experience different kinds of movements in these early years, the senses of movement and balance steadily mature over the first seven years.

Moving freely during the early years is foundational for successful learning later on. Simple movements while doing home chores, such as gardening, mopping, folding laundry and washing involve moving across from the left half of the body to the right and vice versa. This process develops the vertical midline, which is essential for cognitive learning. Both gross and fine motor skills that allow for such crossing form connections between the right and left brain, which leads to flexible and creative thinking in later years.

Some children show a delayed sense of movement. They bump into people and things. They appear to be clumsy and easily drop something they're holding. They might struggle to hold themselves upright, often slumping or collapsing while standing. As they get older, they are unaware of how things are arranged on their desk and struggle to find their pencil among their materials. Such children benefit from experiences that bring awareness to their physical body. Running and walking are highly beneficial for them. Climbing trees, hiking and swinging help greatly too. It is good for them to experience the heaviness of weight in their body, for example, by carrying grocery bags.

Some children have a poorly developed sense of balance. They fidget with their hands and feet and shift about in their chairs. They never tire of being on a swing and keep spinning around without getting dizzy. They want to keep moving all the time because they feel out of balance in stillness. For such children, it helps when they have opportunities to walk on a tree log, jump on tree stumps, walk on a balancing beam, stand and balance on a curvy board, or have a heavy cushion placed on their lap.

Through movement, children process and assimilate what they encounter in the world. For this reason, they need to move freely and in many different ways. By honouring the child's inner need to move, we enable them to take hold of their bodies and eventually themselves.

What Is the Role of Parents?

From being spiritually united with their environment, a child, by constantly interacting with it physically (through eating and eliminating, waking and sleeping, touching and exploring, moving and playing), grows and separates from it. The child is at work, rapidly creating and transforming their physical body by using all the impressions that come their way. Some impressions are solid, such as food and water, while others subtle, say, the tone of the parent's voice. A child tries to digest all these impressions. When digestion is successful, the child absorbs a tiny part of the world and grows. When it is not, it causes discomfort. The young child's incredible openness to the world makes the early years a potent foundation for life. The same openness also makes the child vulnerable. How can parents ensure that their child's expansion into the world and contraction to assimilate and grow from it has a healthy dynamic? Through rhythmic parenting.

Chapter 2

Rhythm: A Cradle for Healthy Growth

A young child is like a sponge, soaking up their environment continuously during their waking hours. The child's inner forces, like a sculptor's hands, receive impressions from the environment to form the physical body. Everything in the environment, eating a juicy strawberry, playing with a remote-controlled car, listening to a story, the touch of a wool sweater, the chirping of birds, conversations between adults, the flash of traffic lights, stimulates these inner forces. Just like a sculpture, if something suddenly pushes the sculptor's hands, the sculpture will flatten. If something moves the hands gently, the sculpture will receive a soft impression. The quality of a child's environment creates soft or hard, slow or sudden impressions on the physical body. What happens when the child receives very strong or too many impressions?

Today, young children are increasingly encountering experiences that are new on the human stage and questionable in terms of their impact on child development. Little children in strollers glued to smartphones in a shopping mall. Three-year-olds expected to write the alphabet at an age when their wrist bones have not developed yet. Four-year-olds being asked to choose the school they want to go to. Hi-tech creep, premature academic expectations and children being treated like little adults are burdensome on a young child. Such experiences demand the child to exercise their feelings and thoughts, which is a premature expectation. (The capacity of feeling starts developing only around seven years of age and of thinking around puberty.) As a result, their formative forces are pulled away from physical growth, which is the actual task of early childhood, and diverted towards dealing with these advanced impressions. Physical development is neglected, formative forces are depleted and the child is saddled with undigested impressions. The result is 'difficult children' when the child is simply expressing their discomfort.

The rhythmic environment of Ukti's kindergarten worked therapeutically on such children. Initially, they found the calm, harmonious mood unsettling. With no intense impressions to drown their unease, they did not know what to do with themselves. They didn't know how to listen to a story without interrupting. They could not enter into free play so they kept moving, talking and disrupting other children's game. They would get cranky easily and cling to the teacher.

When they received the right environment that prioritized their physical development, they started to heal. The process took time—several weeks, even months. Bit by bit, they were freed from the shackles that had been holding them back. They were able to eat well, play by themselves and with other children, sleep well at night and be energetic and joyful during the day. Because they felt at ease with themselves, they were able to take an interest in the world: explore, interact, engage and learn from it.

What was special about this environment that gave children what they needed for their healthy development? It offered them impressions that they could use for their growth and rest that allowed them to digest these impressions.

We make a vessel from a lump of clay; it is the empty space within that makes it useful.

We make doors and windows for a room; But it is these empty spaces that make the room liveable.

Thus, while the tangible has advantages, it is the intangible that makes it useful.[1]

The intangible aspect of growth is rest. The sculptor's hands must pause after stretching. Rest is essential for growth to happen. This is seen most easily with an infant. Drinking milk, the main growth experience, is such intense work for them that they doze off soon after and sometimes even during it. Upon waking, they are energized and ready for the next meal. Activity and rest alternate to create a rhythm of growth.

When we sow a seed, it doesn't turn into a plant overnight. The seed needs to go through the rhythms of the sun, rain and soil, as well as the absence of these forces which allows for their absorption. Then it begins to sprout. This alternating process of activity and rest

---

[1] Lao Tzu, *Tao Teh Ching*. Translated by John C.H. Wu, Shambhala Publications, 1989.

must continue for the sapling to turn into a blossoming plant that bears fruit.

All nature moves and transforms itself in rhythm: the alternation of day and night, the transition from winter to spring, the disappearance and return of comets in the night sky. It is no different for human beings.

Until not very long ago, our lives pulsated to the rhythms of nature. People woke up at the break of dawn and went to sleep after sunset. Spring and summer were active seasons, and things slowed down in autumn and winter. Children played and rested according to these natural rhythms. They rolled about in the dirt, climbed trees and splashed in streams. Their toys were sticks and stones, wooden animals, and simple dolls made of cotton, wool or straw. The child's physical being imbibed impressions from the natural world and grew and developed out of them. Because the natural world moves in predictable rhythms, the child did too. The first sign appeared around three months of age, when babies started sleeping for longer stretches during the night. This was the beginning of the twenty-four-hour circadian rhythm of light and dark—our internal rhythm that is responsible for the healthy functioning of life processes, from digestion to memory consolidation to hormone release and more.

What started with the invention of the light bulb a hundred years ago has metamorphosed into a high-speed train with no brakes. With our technological achievements, we are no longer dependent on nature. The rising and setting of the sun have little bearing on our schedules. We have the freedom to eat, bathe, exercise, work, socialize and sleep at our will. Nature no longer exclusively determines when we are active and when we are at rest. So we can spend hours in our cars, on the phone and in front of our screens, and not even realize. And our children are right there with us. Can they assimilate all these myriad, new experiences for growth?

A child fashions their growth instinctively out of their environment with no control over the environment itself. Today, parents have the unique responsibility of creating the environment and crafting the cradle for their child's healthy growth. This cradle is rhythm.

Crafting the Cradle

When the child's environment is imbued with rhythm, their growth will have the same quality. Parents can create this environment by working with four questions.

1. How does your child experience a typical day?

Any experience has one of two qualities: stretching or releasing. The first experience is asking the child to stretch in order to take something in from the world. We call it an inbreath. These experiences press upon the child's physical organism and stimulate it, and the child grows by assimilating them.

Inbreath

From the time the child wakes up, they begin to breathe in the world: the chirping of birds, the bark of the dog, the aroma of breakfast being cooked, the sight of parents drinking tea, morning hugs and conversations.

Take a moment to reflect on your morning today. Can you identify all the different things that were going on? Start with the obvious ones and list them. Recall anything that you perceived with your senses of sight, sound, touch, smell and taste. They are tangible and easier to remember. Now try and recall how you felt. Did you have any strong emotions? What about your partner? What was the general mood? Was there an unexpected phone call or work email? Something in the news?

Fill out this table to take stock of your morning. Note both what was in the environment and what you added to it:

Sense impressions
Sights:
Sounds:

Smells:

Tastes:

Touch:

Soul impressions
Your feelings:
Your partner's mood:
Other:

Once you're done with this exercise, give yourself a pat on the back. You have just finished characterizing the entire morning. You are now acutely aware of what you experienced. Because your child shares the same environment, you also have a window into their experience, what they absorbed in the first hours of the day—their first inbreath.

If your child goes to day care or kindergarten, they will breathe in more impressions: obvious ones like snacks and meals, rhymes and stories, and less obvious ones like the colours of the classroom, the teacher's tone of voice. All instructions are inbreaths. These could be academic instructions about letters and numbers or instructions for a crafting activity. Then there are impressions a child receives from their peers: 'I will get a kitten for my birthday'; 'My father went to London. He is coming back today, and I will pick him up from the airport'; 'My dog runs away with all the shoes in our house'.

Outbreath

Along with all this stretching activity, the child also receives outbreaths. The outbreath is when the sculptor's hands can be still because no external impression is pushing them, allowing the child's body to process previous stretching experiences and giving the 'hands' a break so they can rest and rejuvenate. Any time the child is moving (running about the house, walking to the car, running about in the playground, playing tag with friends), the child is able to breathe out. The extent of outbreath depends on how long and how freely the child is engaged in movement. Indoor free play also offers the child an opportunity to exhale. If the child has time to be in nature, they have the fullest opportunity to exhale. A nap or quiet time during the day helps digest experiences from the morning. And finally night-time sleep is the ultimate outbreath. All that the child explores and learns during the day is digested in sleep, making it possible for them to resume their task—growing and inhabiting their physical body—the next day.

Both the work of taking in the world during the day and the movement and rest to assimilate it develop the physical body and the senses. Growth happens in a twenty-four-hour continuum. If a child has too much inbreath, they will have a greater need to move and rest. If this need is not met, they will find it difficult to fall asleep at night, making them tired the next day and compromising their ability to take up the task of growth.

2. How long is the child engaged in inbreath versus outbreath experiences?

Take a moment to breathe in and hold your breath. How does it make you feel? Suffocated, right? Now, try breathing out without inhaling. You will be gasping for air in no time. This is why inbreath and outbreath experiences need to alternate rhythmically for the young child to experience harmonious growth.

The table below shares some typical inbreath and outbreath experiences that young children encounter today.

Inbreath Experiences	Outbreath Experiences
Infants and Toddlers (0–2.5 years)	
Nursing or drinking milk	Morning nap
Eating solid foods	Afternoon nap
Being awake	Night-time sleep
Listening to music	Play time, tummy time
Listening to a story	
Screentime	

Preschoolers (2.5–4.5 years) and Kindergarteners (4.5–7 years)	
Eating	Daytime nap
Preschool/Daycare/Kindergarten	Quiet time
Reading books	Cuddle time
Writing	Night-time sleep
Homework	Free, unstructured play (outdoor and indoor)
Loud and crowded settings such as cinema, malls, play zones	Free artistic activity (drawing, painting, clay or playdough)
Social events like weddings, birthday parties	Home chores
Screentime	Time in nature
Extracurricular/after-school classes	

As you think about your child's day, do you find that one or the other experience dominates their day? Is your child mostly breathing in or breathing out? Use this blank table to jot down the inbreaths and outbreaths in your child's typical day. Also add any activities not stated above.

Inbreaths (time spent):	Outbreaths (time spent):

Typically, as the child moves from breakfast to getting ready to driving to school, the inner quality of their experience is not changing. The child is absorbing one impression after another. It would also not be misplaced to say that the child is mostly breathing in at school. As a result, by afternoon, most children have been engaged in one long, unbroken inbreath. Perhaps the first opportunity for release is the afternoon nap. But sometimes the nap gets canned for logistical reasons (a guest drops in, there's an urgent errand to be run, the child is giving a hard time and refusing to nap). Even after the child naps, they need more outbreath. So, if they are packed off in the car to go to an extracurricular class rather than walking to the neighbourhood park to run around and play, the child continues to breathe in rather than receive a proper outbreath.

On the flip side, occasionally, a child ends up with one long, unbroken outbreath. This typically happens when the family heads out for a day in the park. The child keeps playing and running around and barely stops to eat. By the end, the child is completely spent and falls asleep on the ride back home, likely missing their dinner. This might cause them to wake up in the middle of the night, hungry or too tired to fall back to sleep. The next day, they might continue to be tired and cranky.

In both examples above, too much inbreath or outbreath gives the day a jerky quality. In addition, our fast-paced lives require the child's day to be planned according to school schedules, work schedules and other logistical reasons rather than the child's developmental need for rhythm. This leaves the child exposed to powerful forces outside their control and, for that matter, adult control. Children are being asked to know the world as the world swirls chaotically around them, almost akin to getting to know the sea through choppy waves.

3. Could an outbreath experience end up as inbreath for a child?

Yes. Sometimes an outbreath experience can feel like an inbreath because of adult influence.

While free play and movement offer excellent outbreath activities during the day, these gifts can be received by the child only when the activities are not punctuated by instructions and comments from an adult. Similarly, outdoor play is a very healthy outbreath, but a sports class is less so, because the child has to pay attention to the rules of the game and follow instructions from the coach. Clay modelling, which is a wonderful component of play time, can become an inbreath if accompanied by instructions to create this or that shape or animal. The same is true for drawing and painting. Complex, right? How can parents tell if an activity is impressing the world upon the child or allowing them to process the world? The key lies in observing the child during the activity. Is the child mostly following instructions to meet a goal or are they engaging freely out of their inner will?

4. How to craft a rhythmic day for your child?

From the chart you made above, you know whether your child has extended inbreaths or outbreaths in a day. To bring a more rhythmic quality to their day, follow these steps.

The non-negotiables

First tackle the non-negotiables: mealtimes and sleep. A child who eats well and gets plenty of rest during the day and night will begin each day on a solid footing. If you can only do one of these, work on sleep, as it is the ultimate breathing out experience. Usually, the time a child spends outside home, in a kindergarten or day care can largely be considered as an inbreath, so once the child returns home, also make space for naptime or quiet time.

<u>Put anchors in place</u>

Smoothly transitioning the child from inbreath to outbreath and vice versa is key to maintaining a consistent daily rhythm—for instance, leaving the playground on time to be home for dinner. When this doesn't happen, the child ends up breathing in or breathing out too much. Every parent knows how challenging this can be.

This is where anchors come in. Anchors are short experiences that signal a change of course from one breath to another to the child. The anchor must have two parts to it: (1) The child having to do something and (2) the adult leading them into the anchor activity with a simple song.

Simply telling the child to pack up their toys because it's time for dinner is ineffective in this phase of childhood. Instead, when the adult starts with a song and puts a sand toy away, the child imitates and follows along. When this is done every time the child visits the playground, the child builds a physical memory of the transition. Over time, the child comes to expect it and transitions without a peep.

Anchors maintain the daily rhythm as a flow where the child is not jolted out of one major experience to the next. They honour the fact that the child is in a state of oneness with the world around them. For the child, to suddenly snap out of what they're doing is difficult. Anchors allow the child to travel smoothly between the different islands in the day.

Be consistent

Once a rhythm is formed, it needs to be repeated in a consistent manner. Otherwise, for a child it can feel like going from calm seas to high tides from one day to the next, unsettling for them and unconducive to their growth.

Creating a daily rhythm is one thing and sticking to it is quite another. It can take a month or longer to put a rhythm in place. Knowing that it will take time will help you keep at it. The good news is that once you can sustain it for a few weeks, your child will begin to internalize it and moving from one experience to the next will not entirely be on you. When the day unfolds in the same manner each day, your child will come to expect it and ask for it.

Observe your child to make room for changes in their rhythm

While a breathing rhythm is essential for healthy growth, the rhythm needs to change as children grow and develop capacities for absorbing and digesting new impressions. An infant's day has the quality of a mountain stream with short, frequent waves of activity and rest, while a five-year-old's day is more like a river with slightly bigger waves. This trend continues with age. Big waves take longer to rise and recede so an eight-year-old can be engaged in an inbreath, such as doing their homework, and in an outbreath, like playing outdoors, for a longer time than a four-year-old and not get cranky. These outward behaviours are reflected in the body's physiology. Both the breathing rate and the heart rate start off very high at birth and gradually slow down, stabilizing around nine years of age and staying there throughout adult life. As we step into our final years, the breathing rate begins to slow down, an expression of the body's wisdom of preparing for its last outbreath.

The parent's observation is critical to recognizing the need for a new rhythm. A child who has been taking long afternoon naps may no longer require the same as they grow up. They may keep rolling on the bed and gazing at the ceiling and not fall asleep all afternoon. They may need a shorter nap or just quiet time. Alternatively, the child may nap for a longer time if they are going through a growth spurt. As rhythm creates growth, growth requires new rhythms over time.

Other factors can also throw off a child's rhythm. When a child is ill, more rest will be needed.

In this sense, a rhythm is inherently different from a routine in that it is not rigid. A 2 p.m. naptime can extend to 2.30 p.m. but not stretch as far as 3 p.m. Rhythm flows in time but is not limited by it. Rhythm gives the child's day a musical quality.

The Twin Gifts of Rhythm: Confidence and Inner Discipline

When a child experiences the same rhythm on a daily basis, knowing what follows next, it gives them a sense of well-being and strengthens their sense of life. When the day unfolds in the same manner each day, they are freed from the burden of uncertainty and can transition smoothly from one activity to the next without struggle. If the child lays the table before dinner every day, they will know when dinnertime is approaching and will be inwardly ready for it. If they brush their teeth right before putting on their nightclothes every day, they will not need reminders and after some time even initiate the brushing activity on their own. This predictability in their outside environment makes the child feel safe, secure and confident and does away with tantrums that stem from unexpected changes.

Rhythm also serves as an inherent form of discipline where the need for external, coercive measures becomes redundant. Rhythm carries them through the day without the need for the adult to remind them multiple times, 'It's time to brush your teeth', or 'You must go to bed, it's late'. Rhythm is a boundary that gently tugs at the child when they stray too far. A consistent, breathing rhythm helps parents do away with typical forms of discipline, like carrot and stick, reasoning or negotiations.

Frequently Asked Questions

1. After my child gets home from preschool or day care, should he have inbreath or outbreath?

   Ans: While the child may have some outbreath experiences during their time at the kindergarten or day care, like playtime, in relation to them, the inbreath experiences dominate. So, once the child returns home, there can be a short inbreath where they eat a snack followed by a longer outbreath: a nap or quiet time.

2. When does drawing, painting or clay modelling become an inbreath experience for the child?

   Ans: Drawing, painting, modelling and other kinds of art can be wonderful ways for the child to digest prior inbreath experiences. However, if the child is given a picture book in which they have to fill colour within a form, it becomes a breathing-in experience. It is the same if the child draws/paints in an after-school class in a guided way, with instructions. On the other hand, if the child is handed a blank page to explore and engage with colours, it is an outbreath experience.

3. What are some signs that my child's day lacks a rhythm?

   Ans: Here are some tell-tale signs that a child's day lacks a rhythm:

   - The child is cranky during the day.
   - The child throws frequent tantrums and has meltdowns over trivial things.
   - The child is fussy about food or clothes.
   - It is difficult to get your child to do regular things, like brushing their teeth, putting on their shoes or getting ready for school.
   - The child resists going to bed.
   - The child has difficulty waking up in the morning on their own.
   - The child is lethargic during the day.

- The child talks a lot or moves about constantly and is unable to calm down and rest.
- The child is unable to engage in play.

4. We are working parents to a four-year-old. Our schedules are erratic. How do we begin to create a rhythm?

   Ans: Start with the non-negotiables: mealtimes, snack times, nap times and bedtime, and fix their time in the daily rhythm. To help your child transition to these non-negotiables, place an anchor before each of them. By engaging in the anchor activity, the child remembers and becomes inwardly ready to start the main activity, say dinner time. The key is to do this consistently.

5. It is a challenge to make my five-year-old go from one thing to the next. I have to repeatedly tell her before she finds her way to dinner or is ready for bedtime. What should I do to make things go more smoothly?

   Ans: This behaviour can stem from a number of reasons:
   - First, observe your child to determine if they are overstimulated or tired during the day. Modify the

rhythm to create a balance between outbreath and inbreath activities.

- Involve your child in creating a rhythm chart that can be put up on the fridge or some common space. Encourage them to draw on it so they can make it their own. Refer to this chart next time. Since the child has been involved in making the chart, they will be keen to know what's next.
- Finally, insert anchors in the rhythm to ease transitions.

6. When we travel on a holiday, our routine goes haywire. What can we do to ensure that when we return, it is easier for our child to adjust to the home routine?

Ans: While it is not possible to maintain the same rhythm on a holiday or on visits to the grandparents' place, what helps the child find some balance when they are away from home is to hold the non-negotiable aspects of the rhythm strongly: mealtimes, rest times and sleep times. Maintaining this core part of the rhythm will help the child adjust quickly upon returning home.

7. I have a three-year-old and I work from home. I struggle with syncing our rhythms. When I have to work, it's his playtime and he wants me there. So, I let him watch the screen instead. What can I do?

   Ans: Playtime is an essential outbreath for the child and integral to maintaining balance in your child's day. Treat playtime as sacred and make an arrangement for someone to be with your child while they play with their toys or in the park. It is far better for the child to play under someone else's care than to replace their playtime with screen time.

8. We are working parents to a six-year-old. When we return home, we like to spend time with our child. But then it becomes difficult to put her to bed because she is wide awake. What should we do?

   Ans: It can be hard to make this choice. However, it is important to remember what the child needs at this age. Maintaining a daily rhythm is foundational for the child's lifelong health. When the child's meal and sleep times are postponed in order to accommodate adult schedules, it throws several things off: digestion of food, assimilation of the day's experiences, rest and rejuvenation of the child's formative forces, and for all these reasons, the rhythm for the next day, which will make the child cranky, lethargic and prone to meltdowns. For working parents, early morning, before leaving for work and school, is the best time for the family to spend time together. This way, the child receives your warm and loving attention to start their day and their bedtime is not compromised.

9. My partner and I are separated, and our child splits their time between two homes. How can we maintain a rhythm for our child?

    Ans: Separation can be a difficult experience for a child. What helps is if both parents can commit to the same rhythm for their child in their separate homes. If not all aspects can be maintained, it is effective to keep the mealtime, naptime and bedtime rhythm the same and to limit intense inbreath experiences, like screen use. By minimizing overstimulation, the child is able to transition from one home to the other with more ease.

10. Things are pretty smooth during the week, but it is very hard to maintain our child's rhythm over the weekend. What can we do?

Ans: Again, it is really important to stick to the non-negotiables: mealtimes, rest times and sleep times on the weekend. When this core rhythm is maintained, the child finds it easy to transition to the week.

Chapter 3
Screen Time: An Intense Inbreath

In our many years of work with children, and from being parents ourselves, we have realized that screen use is the most powerful inbreath for children of any age, especially young ones. When screen use becomes a part of the daily rhythm, it doubly undermines childhood. Young children, with sponge-like impressionability, have to work hard to digest the powerful impressions they receive from the screen. At the same time, screen use eats into experiences that are critical for their task of developing the physical body and the senses. Children miss out on foundational experiences while being saddled with advanced impressions they struggle to process. The rest of the chapter breaks down this double whammy.

Distorted Influence on Organ Development

Young children are constantly taking in impressions from their environment. What this environment includes and what the child does with these impressions is most profound.

> What goes on in his physical environment, this the child imitates, and in the process of imitation his physical organs are cast into forms which then become permanent. 'Physical environment' must, however, be taken in the widest imaginable sense. It includes not only what goes on around the child in the material sense, but everything that takes place in the child's environment—everything that can be perceived by his senses, that can work from the surrounding physical space upon the inner powers of the child. This includes all moral or immoral actions, all wise or foolish actions, that the child sees.
>
> —Rudolf Steiner[1]

---

[1] Rudolf Steiner, 'The Education of the Child in the Light of Anthroposophy' (Translated by George and Mary Adams), The Rudolf Steiner Archive, 1927, available at: https://rsarchive.org/Articles/GA034/English/Singles/EduChi_essay.html (accessed 13 February 2025).

What does it mean for this physical development if a good chunk of what children see and hear comes from the screen? The development of good sight requires the right conditions of light and colour. Does the screen provide these? What about the impact of electronic sound on the developing sense of hearing? An honest look at any children's programme will tell us that it prioritizes entertainment over child development.

Shrinkage of Movement, Growth and Learning

When children have plenty of opportunities for free movement, they learn about their environment, develop their body and senses, all of which become the foundation for later learning.

When they're out in the park, they might encounter a grasshopper. They run after it and try to catch it. As they look at it and feel it on their palm, they gain an understanding of the grasshopper. They develop their sense of touch and sight in the process. When the grasshopper hops off and flies away, they gain a sense of movement. Later, you might find them hopping around in the living room. When children spend most of their free time in front of the screen rather than moving about and exploring, they are being robbed of this education.

By its highly stimulating impact, a screen grips a young child with fast-moving images. Instead of being busy moving about themselves, the child is relegated to a passive consumption of two-dimensional motion. It is like taking away all the paints and brushes from a master artist and locking them in a room full of paintings on the walls. It is no surprise then that many children today struggle to jump rope or have coordinated movements.

The screen is a colossal shrinkage of the world it tries to depict. Shrinkage of 3D visual reality to 2D images on a rectangle. Shrinkage of a world of infinite sounds to a handful. Shrinkage of real sound to electronic sound. When screen time substitutes for lived experiences, children's senses can remain underdeveloped. Watching the most beautiful rose on the screen can never take the place of holding it in your hands to feel its presence. A child who routinely watches something while eating misses out on fully knowing the food through its textures, colours, sounds, smell and taste. What a pity if the crunch of a fresh carrot is never fully registered by the child because they are engrossed in what's happening on the screen.[2]

---

[2] The same is true when a picture book is shown to a child while feeding them, only to a lesser degree.

We cannot be people of this world if we have not had enough opportunities, especially during our formative years, to engage with the real world. Today, we have an urgent need to wake up to this truth as the influx of digitization, coupled with AI, has nearly eliminated the need for direct interactions with the world around us.

If Truth Begets Trust, Falsity Begets Mistrust

Young children feel at one with the world, see the world as good and trust it completely. This is why they happily put mud in their mouths only to spit it out a few moments later when it tastes unpalatable. By sensing the world, they come to know it. What happens when much of the world comes to them through the screen? Here's an anecdote about a child in Ukti's kindergarten:

> He found a caterpillar in the garden and was overjoyed. This was soon replaced by worry. The child looked disturbed. He told his mother that the caterpillar was unwell; it was too small and thin and needed to eat more food. With help from his mother, the little boy made a

house for the caterpillar using a shoebox and put some leaves in it for the caterpillar to eat. This went on for a few days, but the child had trouble sleeping at night. He went to his mother crying, 'I keep feeding my caterpillar, but it looks ill. It is not even opening its eyes! ' The mother reassured him that the caterpillar was fine. But the child was implacable. 'I saw on TV how big and fat caterpillars are. They have big eyes too. Is my caterpillar dying?'

The child had been watching a show with a large, googly-eyed caterpillar that bounced about on the screen. Compared to it, the small size and tiny eyes of his own caterpillar has caused the child a great deal of worry.

For a child, contradictory experiences create a feeling of unease. It undermines their innate trust in the world. From an open-armed stance, the child recoils a bit inwardly. And if one screen image can have such an impact, what does routine consumption of thousands of images do to their relationship with the world? How might it affect their curiosity and sense of wonder? How might it affect them as a learner? As they get older, will they be able to view the world as their own, take wholehearted interest in it and be ready to step in and engage?

Interference with Sleep and Metabolism

Have you noticed how many images per minute pass before a child's eyes in a typical children's programme on a screen? For a young child whose nervous system is still very young, watching the screen is highly stimulating. The pace at which the images move is something they cannot process, and the exaggerated sounds of a roaring lion or racing car can be overwhelming. Unlike the real experience of watching the sun set and the moon rise, a smiley sun with roving eyes, gliding across the sky, is a complex experience for a child to digest.

Young children who are regular screen users are in such a nervous, excitable state that they struggle to calm down and relax, just like an elastic band that has been stretched so far, it cannot go back to its regular length. Screen use is a primary reason why many children today have sleep issues. In a 2021 systematic review of ninety-nine studies, researchers found that 'an increased amount of screen exposure leads to adverse sleep outcomes in children and adolescents'.[3] When sleep is inadequate or of poor quality,

---

[3] Sin-Chin Tan, Jenny Fraser - 76 Effects of screen time on sleep in children and adolescents: a systematic review: BMJ Paediatrics Open 2021;5.

the child's metabolism is affected, which shows up as issues with eating and elimination. Finally, a child who is sleep-deprived and nutrient-deficient will struggle to develop a healthy sense of life and often appear restless or lethargic.

Screen Dependance

You are calling your child to come for naptime. Your words fall on deaf ears. You call out repeatedly. Your child doesn't respond. You turn off the show they're watching and they start to bawl. This is a common scenario in most households today. Trying to make the child understand doesn't help. Getting upset with them, even less so. Then negotiations begin, followed by deals: 'I will let you watch for thirty minutes if you go to the playground afterwards.' Now you're on a slippery slope. You have assumed that your child will remember, think logically and exercise self-control, when the truth is that none of these faculties have developed at this age. Soon the parent–child relationship, which is still so young and needs careful tending, is ridden with arguments. Parents steadily lose authority and struggle to get the child to do basic things such as eating and sleeping—experiences that are critically important for health. Over the years, screen dependence grows, and by teenage years, it has major repercussions, being associated with anxiety, mental health issues and poor academic performance.

Premature Consumerization

Online shopping with the click of a button, anything from a toothbrush to a laptop arriving within hours at your doorstep, and targeted ads on every major platform all make shopping ubiquitous and extremely easy. This is the world little children are stepping into right out of the womb. Five-year-olds have their own mobile phones and can order food at the click of a button. Four-year-olds make shopping recommendations to parents, convincing them to buy the latest video game. Over time, with easy access to online phone shopping, children are pulled into consumerism and trained as little shoppers, far before they have reached the maturity to make informed decisions.

Instant Gratification and the Weakening of Will Forces

Within a span of ten minutes, a little girl on the screen rescues her bunny who had gotten lost on a mountain and fallen into a ditch. With the click of a button, a child fills a pre-made sketch on their tablet with bright, beautiful colours. With one yell at the smart speaker, a three-year-old gets to play their favourite song. What is common across these scenes? Things happen quickly, without much effort, and the results are fabulous. Children's programmes are rife with great challenges being resolved with ease. Children's toys and smart devices are designed to make things convenient with spectacular results at the end.

After repeated experiences of this kind, the child comes to expect instant gratification. At a deeper level, they fail to develop the understanding that it takes effort and many, many steps to make something happen. Because learning takes place through doing in these early years, every time things happen magically for the child without them having to move a finger, they are robbed of a developmental opportunity.

The loss is not immediately evident. Perhaps the child walks away from a drawing they just started or doesn't pick up something they dropped. No big deal. They'll learn as they get older, we tell ourselves. Then come the tantrums about cleaning their play area. The situation finally comes to a head at school. The child struggles to start the task assigned to them, and if they manage to start, they struggle to finish it, abandoning it halfway.

On the other hand, a child who puts their toys away after they're done playing, lays the table and clears it after meals, sows a seed and waters the plant regularly, learns that with their hands they make things happen. They learn that it takes multiple steps to accomplish a task. They understand that they might not succeed in the first attempt, but perseverance will make the result finer each time. They accept that mistakes are part and parcel of getting anything done. Over the years, they build an inner capacity for initiative, diligence, patience and learning. They build a healthy will.

Inhibiting Imagination

Exploring the world through play is the ground on which a child's imagination is born. Screen use hinders this process. Instead of having a direct experience of the world and building their own mental images of a house, a river or an old woman, children passively consume the product of someone else's imagination. Unlike their own images, which are original and unique, and grow with them as they experience the world, screen images are uniform and sophisticated and get fixed in a child's mind. A child who watches regular screen content will draw their house with a sloping roof even if they live in a neighbourhood with high-rise apartment buildings. The screen house is more stimulating and makes a greater impression on them than the real house. Over time, this stunts their imagination.

This is most easily seen during free play. Children with regular screen use are unable to enter play either on their own or with other children, and if they do, they cannot play for long. The screen images in their mind are so powerful that when children are given free time, they keep acting out those images. This, in itself, is a healthy process and sometimes lasts for months. But it happens at the cost of real engagement with the world in two ways. One, the real-world impressions don't even reach the child because the child is so saturated with screen impressions—a desensitization of sorts. Two, when the child does absorb real impressions, they are unable to digest them during play because the screen impressions dominate. Ultimately, the child misses out on the opportunity of free play, during which real-world impressions can become food for their growing imagination.

Children who do not receive the gift of imagination through free play struggle with independent, flexible, out-of-the-box thinking, a necessity in the workplace and in life.

Hindering Socialization

Starting around three years of age, children become developmentally ready to play with another child. As children begin to engage directly with each other, they start their lifelong journey of becoming a social being. Using their physical body and senses as vehicles, they start gaining an understanding of what it is like to be with another human being. This learning has profound implications for life. It is the foundation of all relationships, personal and professional. A child who is a regular screen user will struggle to play with other children. Meanwhile, a child who is given ample opportunities to play with other children will develop key capacities of trust, empathy, boundaries, judgement and love that will enable them to have healthy relationships later.

Social capacities built during play are also foundational for learning. Children learn best with their peers. However, if a child is unable to have ongoing interactions with their peers, their learning is compromised. Down the road, they will struggle with teamwork and leadership.

How can a child develop social capacities when screen use directly cuts into time spent playing with other children? How can a child who is imitating adults around them learn to be social when adult interactions are happening largely on the screen?

Frequently Asked Questions

1. How can you help reduce the overstimulating impact of screen use on your child?

   Ans: If your child is a regular screen user, irrespective of the type of content they watch or the duration, it is an intense inbreath experience for the child and burdens their developing senses. Here's what you can do:

   - The first thing to do before you can wean them off the screen is to introduce and make time for outbreath experiences, free play being the most effective, to process screen content.
   - Doing home chores such as kneading dough to make bread or roti, moulding clay or playdough, and spending time in nature are other experiences

that help the child calm the overstimulated nervous system. Start by adding one of these activities on the weekends, as it may be hard to include them on weekdays initially. However, once you start, commit to doing it with your child every weekend at the same time. This way, the child will anticipate the activity and take it up with vigour and interest, making your job easier as a parent. Gradually, you can bring these changes into the week as well.

2. Does the type of content matter?

Ans: Before you can wean your child off the screen, start regulating the content they watch.

- First of all, stop watching any shows with violence. This could be as (seemingly) harmless as a cat hitting a mouse with a frying pan.
- Next, remove any instructional content. This includes educational, moralistic and religious content.
- Finally, discard any content that is emotional or dramatic. Exaggerated and unrealistic sounds with caricatures or fantastical characters all fall under this category. A young child does not understand

emotions and drama, so when they are exposed to such content, their bodies struggle to absorb these strong impressions.

- Choose content that has soft colour tones, gentle yet articulate speech and images that are close approximations of reality.

3. What is one thing parents can do to reduce screen dependence in their children?

   Ans: Young children imitate everything that happens in their environment. So one thing parents can do when children are around is to avoid using their phone or laptop. This can be very hard at first, especially since people work from home and the phone has become necessary for completing so many small and big tasks from morning till night. However, little by little, parents need to start establishing screen-free hangout times with their child. Even if this is only fifteen minutes to begin with, it will be the start of a healthy family habit. Over time, the duration can be increased.

   Parents will also realize and appreciate how the quality of time spent together with their child is vastly better without the screen. And children will start to realize that the screen is not an essential part of their childhood and their world, which will become the foundation for their healthy relationship with devices.

4. How can screen hours be minimized for a child?

   Ans: Children today are exposed to screens everywhere, whether it is at home and school, in restaurants and malls, in game zones and cinema halls, or at their friend's place. While it is beyond the purview of parents to avoid screen exposure at school, they can still exercise screen avoidance, for example, when choosing a restaurant. They can plan trips to the mall and cinema hall when their child is not in their care.

   By becoming conscious of the amount of screen time the child is receiving, parents will be able to cut out non-essential exposure.

5. How can we wean the child off the screen?

   Ans: This will be a process and the child will need to be held with empathy and love as well as clear and consistent boundaries as you try to wean them. Here are a few things you can start with:

   - Identify the times when the child uses the screen at home.

- Start with eliminating screen use during free time and fill this time with experiences that engage the will and imagination of the child, for instance, home chores, clay modelling, drawing, painting, free play and so on.
- Since the child is used to watching the screen during free time, it will be difficult for them to switch to a new activity. They will need to be hand-held. For this, you will need to initiate the activity, say kneading dough, so that the child can follow by imitating you.
- Then, start to eliminate screen use during mealtimes. This will take longer and may seem difficult at first. Instead of watching something, tell them a story from your childhood or a puppy you saw on the way back from work. Eventually, your child will learn to eat without the need to be distracted by a screen.

6. How much screen time is okay for children up to seven years?

   Ans: The answer is simple: none. As adults around the young child, we encourage you to strive towards this ideal. Be kind to yourself and remember that this transition will need time. You are dealing with evermore sophisticated technology that is being pushed into every corner of our lives.

But as a human being, you have the freedom to say no, to use your judgement about where screens are essential and where they are not. So, for example, occasional video calls to keep in touch with a parent who's travelling or with grandparents who live far away are meaningful exceptions to the rule.

As you exercise this mindfulness, you will feel empowered and your child will benefit not just from the outward results of putting the screen genie back in the bottle but also from your constant striving.

7. What to do when your child throws a tantrum to watch something?

   Ans: A tantrum about screen time is no different than one about a bag of chips. Both experiences are designed to be enticing and habit-forming. When you remember this and the fact that screen use has a detrimental effect on your child's health and development, it will help you hold your ground, knowing that you have your child's best interest in mind.

It is important to not lose your temper. Your child has done nothing wrong. They are simply expressing a screen habit. So, you need to hold your ground, with love.

Acknowledge your child's response as real. You can say, 'I know you want to watch (name of their favourite show), but the iPad is tired and has gone to sleep.' Don't bother using logical reasoning; it doesn't work with young children. (In fact, this faculty does not start developing until about twelve years of age!)

A warm hug, a gentle rub and a repetition of your stand is enough. You can hum a tune that is soothing for your child and keep the conversation to a minimum. Hold them as they cry. Meanwhile, start an activity such as moulding clay which will help channel their energy. Do not invite your child to join. Simply, place a ball of clay next to them and keep working on your own clay. Eventually, they will follow along.

8. How can you host a screen-free play date for your child with their friend?

    Ans: When your child goes to their friend's place for a play date, they often watch a cartoon or something else, there's popcorn and treats, and they may even play for a bit. Your child always comes back excited and happy. If you are a parent striving towards a screen-free childhood for your child, invite your child's friend over and try these ideas:

- Bring some bedsheets and make a tent along with the children. Put some cushions, dolls and kitchen toys, some blocks and let them play.
- Bake some cookies with them. Later they can have a tea party in their tent house.
- Take them to the park and let them run around and play in the sand and dirt. Carry some sand toys along.
- If you live close to a forest or hill, have a picnic outdoors. Let them walk, climb trees, hike and rough it out.

9. How does habitual screen use affect children beyond the early years?

   Ans: When children are exposed to electronic media in their early years, they continue to suffer harmful effects throughout their school years. Here are some challenges that we as educators notice among children on a regular media diet:

- They struggle to learn independently at school and need a lot of support from teachers and parents. This usually means additional homework and stress for the child and parents.
- They have difficulty making friends. They have difficulty picking up social cues, understanding and empathizing with people around them, and maintaining friendships.
- They are disinterested in the real world—a barrier to learning.
- They get bored easily—a barrier to learning because they cannot maintain their focus.
- They have trouble starting an assignment as well as finishing it. So, they lag behind their peers.

10. What to do when your child says, 'My friends keep watching movies and TV shows. Why can't I?'

    Ans: There will always be something others do or have that your child feels they lack. Friends could be wearing expensive clothes, having fancy birthday parties, sleeping late in the night, eating junk food and more. Not watching the screen is just one of the many things your child might be doing differently. The screen is more accessible so your child will be more persistent with their demands on this one. Here's what you can do as a parent:

- Every family has their values and customs and creating one about the screen is no different. Children feel safe and secure when parents establish clear boundaries for them. Don't shy away from or feel guilty about protecting your child. Simply say to your child, 'This is how we do it in our home. Your friend's parents decide what they do in their home.' This is enough for the child. Home is their anchor and over time they will understand. Sometimes a nature story helps. Something along the lines of eagles live in mountaintops, soaring high in the sky, while squirrels live in tree trunks and burrow in the ground to store their food. Your child will understand that people live in different ways and gradually will learn to embrace difference and become comfortable in their own skin.
- Stick to the boundaries you have established. There will be resistance anytime you try to set a boundary. Don't worry. Whining and crying are natural responses from a child. You can acknowledge their

discomfort with a little nod, saying, 'I know this is hard for you.' Give them a hug. If they start crying again, comfort them. But don't give in.

- Practise boundaries consistently every day. When you do this, your child will slowly develop a habit of not watching the screen. You will not need a carrot-and-stick approach. You will avoid coercion, which makes parents feel guilty afterwards. You will also avoid losing your authority with your child, which happens when you bribe them to make them do things.
- Engage your child with screen-free activities. Let your child share these activities with their friends on the next play date.

Chapter 4

The Place of Education in the Rhythm of Growth

Trying to understand how young children are growing and developing is incomplete without a look at education. Around the world, the majority of children below seven years spend the first half of their day outside their home. Some start around five years in kindergarten, some around three in nursery and some start younger, at one or two years, in a day care.

Why are little ones going outside their homes, away from their parents and family, on a daily basis? One reason is obvious: to find care because they have working parents. This is the original reason in fact. Care centres for children under seven began very recently in human history when factory workers in eighteenth-century Europe needed a place to leave their young ones as more and more men and women had to find full-time employment to survive.

But there is more to it. Children go to preschool even when care is available at home. The reason we typically hear is 'for learning'. There is a feeling that the earlier a child starts learning letters and numbers, the better prepared they will be for their academic journey. The feeling is reaffirmed by the plethora of educational toys that send the message 'the sooner, the better'. A quick online search reveals some bestsellers: microscopes for five-year-olds, a busy book on which a three-year-old can stick velcro flash cards of letters, numbers, shapes and even planets, and flash cards that talk to toddlers at the press of a button about apples, helicopters and everything in between. Not to be left behind, infants have their own bestseller: a piggy bank that teaches numbers, colours and Spanish words when fed with coins.

The message is reinforced when preschools start to teach reading and writing and the teacher expresses concern that the four-year-old is struggling to write the alphabet and parents must work with their child at home. As parents figure out how to get their child to learn, more questions arise. Might an after-school reading and writing class help? Is once a week enough? Should I enrol my child for math enhancement as well? What about keeping the child busy on other days of the week? Would a sports class or music lesson be a good choice?

When other children are enrolled in two, three, sometimes four different classes, parents feel the pressure to conform. Conversations with peer parents serve as routine reminders of something more the child could be doing. After all, there are twenty-four hours in a day and the more spent on learning, the better.

Where is the child in all of this? Is the original need for sending them out of the house being fulfilled? Are they receiving the care they deserve? Is their primary task in early childhood being honoured? Are they able to grow and develop their physical body and senses through education? Before we turn to these questions, let's consider for a moment what life was like for little children before the invention of preschools.

Life Before Preschools

What were children doing in their first seven years of life before preschools were a thing? If we could travel back in time and be a fly on the wall, we might see scenes like this. A two-year-old boy sleeping in a basket on his mother's back as she plucks leaves in a tea garden. A four-year-old helping his grandma shell peas for dinner, opening the green pods with his tiny fingers and carefully emptying the peas into the bowl, one by one. A six-year-old girl helping her father take care of the family's horses, bathing and feeding them. A whole bunch of children racing down a dirt hill to play in the nearby stream, with the little ones trailing behind. Another group of children playing while their mothers, aunts and grandmas beat down on red chillies with long pestles, swaying and humming to the grinding rhythm. A little one getting tired of playing and running to her mother to find comfort and rest.

These and similar vignettes are still alive in many parts of the world today. What is common across them? First, the child is engaged with the world around them through their physical body, through the large movements of their arms and limbs and through the tiny movements of their fingers and toes (yes, you use your toes to run downhill or to pluck fruit from a branch!). Not only are these children gaining physical awareness, becoming strong in their bodies and experiencing healthy growth, they are also developing a solid sense of movement and balance. Second, being in natural surroundings and among humans and animals offers a variety of impressions that help children develop their physical senses.

And lastly, other than the occasional hand holding to keep them away from danger, children are largely free to alternate between stretching and resting. Within the larger rhythm of the family, the child, depending on their own nature, finds their rhythm of inbreath and outbreath. One child might be constantly moving and exploring, while another might do that for a bit before sitting down to play with a toy. A third child might run to her mother and sit in her lap. A fourth child, who has been following his older siblings, gets overwhelmed and starts crying, at which point the mother or some other adult picks him up and comforts him. Let's try to understand these four scenarios in terms of inbreath and outbreath.

| First child | This child has a capacity for a longer inbreath. They are able to keep taking in sense impressions from their environment and keep looking for more. |

Second child	The second one is done a bit sooner and settles down to play by themselves to process the impressions.
Third child	For the third child, the inbreath stimulated their senses to a greater extent and they immediately sought their mother for rest; they needed a stronger outbreath than play which was enough for the second child.
Fourth child	This little one got ahead of themselves and experienced a temporary sensory overload. Crying is a sign of too much stimulation and a call for an immediate outbreath.

An easy way to picture these children is by age, with the first child being around five or so and each successive child being younger. However, they can also be of the same age, just with different capacities to take in the world. Some can take bigger bites, while others are small eaters. The main thing is that because they are not spending their day according to one fixed curriculum, they have more freedom to breathe in the world according to their individual capacity and step away from the humdrum when tired.

What's Going on in Preschools?

Today, sending children to preschool has become the norm, and when we make this decision, we are choosing the preschool's rhythm for our child. We are choosing a certain set of activities arranged in a certain sequence as the environment for our child's physical development.

Assessing whether a preschool programme supports your child's physical growth and development can seem like a daunting task. Where does one begin? It is hard enough to get full information on exactly what your child does at preschool. How does one try to understand whether what they do is helping or hindering them?

In the table below, we describe two preschools and the main activities children experience in each one. We ask that you read this table as follows:

Step 1: Read the first scenario (Column 1). Jot down how you feel when you put yourself in your child's shoes going through this preschool day.

Step 2: Repeat the same step for the second scenario (Column 2).

Step 3: Read both scenarios again, this time row by row, and ask which version would be a better facilitator of a child's physical development. Remember, physical development needs both activities that invite the child to breathe in sense impressions from their surroundings and assimilate them through movement and rest.

Preschool 1	**Preschool 2**
Outdoor time	
Children go outdoors to play games. An instructor lays out a pattern of plastic hoops on the ground and tells the children to jump through them. Similar structured exercises follow, like jumping jacks or running through an obstacle course.	Children walk to a park or woods near school. Part of the area is flat ground covered with grass, mud or sand. In some spots, there are trees, and birds can be found chirping or flitting about. At certain times of the year, water appears in some form: a stream, a pond, tiny and large puddles.

Sometimes they play games like Simon Says or Duck Duck Goose, and the teacher makes sure they follow the rules. On another day, they go to the school playground (or a neighbourhood park) which has a swing, a slide and a climbing structure. The children start playing on these.	In springtime, flowers appear. They invite bees and butterflies. Later in the year, the ground might be covered with dry autumn leaves. Some children tumble and roll about in the grass, some dig their hands and feet in the sand and pour it all over themselves, and some play with twigs (snapping them, tapping the ground and making shapes in the dirt, and collecting a huge pile of them). Some try to climb a tree or swing from its branch. Others try to balance while walking on a log on the ground.

Teachers instruct the children to stay in the playground and not venture onto the grassy field for safety reasons. On a different day, the children are led to an artificial grass turf outside their classroom. A couple of children throw a ball down a small plastic slide, a little girl rocks back and forth on a plastic horse, and a boy tries to go forward on a plastic scooter.	A few children cannot seem to sit down: they run about, chase each other, climb up a little dirt hill, come hurtling down and then do it all over again. The teacher observes quietly, keeping every child in their purview, and stepping in when needed. Rain arrives a few months later and with it, new possibilities: children make mud balls, jump in and out of puddles, and engineer a bridge of rocks and stems over a stream.
Indoor Free Play	
Children are assigned to different stations. Once they have spent some time playing with materials in that station, the teacher	The toys are all on their respective shelves, and when the teacher sings a song, the children know it's time to play.

floats among the children to bring academic concepts through guided questions. For example, at the first station, children make a drawing with colourful bubble wrap. After they are done, the teacher asks a series of questions: 'Can you count the number of colours you used?'; 'Is that a mountain you have made?' 'What were you thinking about while creating this painting?' At the next station, the children play with a car and town set. Once they create something, the teacher comes by and says: 'Wow! This is a big town. They find their way to different corners depending on their interest or they simply follow another child. In no time, the kindergarten comes alive with the children's imagination. Little wooden cows and horses start grazing, the farmer comes and collects eggs from the chicken coop, and a hen flies to meet a pig who's resting. In the kitchen corner, a tea party is being prepared and wooden vegetables are being chopped to make soup. In a third corner, large pieces of cloth become a castle, where little babies (dolls) are gently put to rest, with a lullaby.

Does it remind you of your own town?' Then the children move to the third station, which has small and large colourful pebbles in a large box. Once the children have spent a few minutes playing with them, the teacher asks, 'Can you sort the pebbles by size, shape and colour? Where do you think these pebbles may have come from? Can you name the colours of the different pebbles? When you see the colour blue, what does it remind you of?' At the last station, the children sit down and work on a table with puzzles like fitting

Hand-knitted yarn strings become a horse's rein as a rider pulls on his 'horse' and trots about. Wooden blocks of different sizes take the shape of a tower, an apartment building, a bridge and so on. In a wooden canopy covered with rainbow cloth, some monkeys can be found hanging and clattering. A 'doctor' checks on a 'patient's' tummy ache, handing him invisible medicine. Two children pick up wooden spoons and start 'shooting' at each other—an outbreath they need for the action movies they've been watching.

numbers and shapes in the correct slot, or with wooden animal puzzles, or they sort plastic vegetables and place like-coloured vegetables in the same basket. Ultimately, indoor play time, which is meant to be a pure outbreath to process previous impressions, becomes an inbreath for the child because it is accompanied with questions, remarks and teaching academic concepts .	Meanwhile, the teacher sits in a corner, busying herself with sewing or knitting something for the classroom, all the while keeping the children in her awareness to make sure that the play remains healthy and safe for all.
Circle Time	
The teacher sits with the children in a circle and asks a series of questions.	The teacher begins with a song: *Winter, winter has come along*

'How are you feeling today?' or 'What did you eat for breakfast?' Some children respond, some stay quiet, while others lie down on their backs and start rolling about (which is quickly followed by the teacher prompting them to sit up and pay attention). The teacher then leads the conversation to an upcoming festival, important public event or a discussion on the environment. The teacher follows this up with a learning review. Children are asked what day of the week it is, and which month it is, how many children are present,	*The days are short and the nights are long* *The birds are flying to a faraway land* *For sunshine has lost its warm golden hand...* The children stand in a circle with the teacher and follow her movements and gestures as they sing along. On their toes, they fly like birds, closing into their bodies when the days are short, and opening wide, with outstretched arms, when the night is long. The circle continues, *A little bird who could hardly fly asked mother birdie, 'Must we go from our warm nest here, can't we stay someplace near?'*

who all are absent, and their task is to go up to a chart on the wall and point at the correct answer.

Mother birdie said to her little one, 'We must fly soon and go far my dear, for grandfather winter is almost here.'

And off 'fly' the children on tiptoes with outstretched arms, round and round in the circle, following their teacher. The words are not childlike; instead, they are steeped in meaning about the world. They are carefully chosen for their quality of bringing the goodness and beauty of the world to the little child. It does not matter if the child does not know their meanings at first;

the meaning will come with repetition as the same circle continues for the next three weeks. What is important at this stage is for the child to live in the sounds and rhythms of language. How an 'O' feels different from an 'A', not just in their mouth, but in their whole body. When they move swiftly like a cat, while saying 'cat', they experience the quality of the word in their whole body.

They feel the difference in language when they lumber like a 'bear' or fly like an 'eagle'. With time, more complicated movements, like crossing the horizontal

	and vertical midlines, are brought to the children which develop cognitive capacities for later academic learning. The circle varies by time of the year. When a festival or change of season is not approaching, the theme switches to traditional professions like those of a cobbler, potter, farmer, blacksmith and so on, accompanied by varied, developmentally important movements, like tapping their fists like a cobbler, stamping their feet like a woodchopper carrying a heavy load and planting the field like a farmer.

	Animals frequently visit these circles and children skip like lambs, scamper like mice, slither like snakes, jump like frogs and lumber like bears. As the circle comes to a close, they curl up and sleep like snails to bring their movements to rest and their breathing to normal.
Chores	
Children do not do chores. Anything that is dirty or broken gets taken care of by the staff and the room appears magically clean when the children return the next day. The children are rarely involved in taking care of their space.	Mealtimes begin with children laying the table, wearing their aprons either with each other's or the teacher's help, and helping the teacher serve the meal by passing bowls to each other. At the end of the meal, they put everything away, wipe the table, and clean and dry the dishes.

	They sweep the floor along with the teacher for any crumbs that may have fallen. Then there are day-wise chores: helping the teachers prepare lunch by cutting, peeling vegetables and fruits, weeding the garden, watering the plants, cleaning the toys and crayons, changing the clothes of the dolls while the teacher mends any toys that need mending, washing the rags used for dusting and mopping and more.
Artistic activity	
Children are handed outline drawings. The teacher instructs the children to colour in the drawings and to be careful not to spill over the lines.	Children are handed plain paper and crayons for drawing. Some will simply scribble and create what looks like a complex web of lines and shapes; others start

Sometimes, teachers will tell the children to use yellow for the sun and green for the trees and so on. In the pottery session, children use clay or playdough to create different shapes with guidance and instructions from the teacher. On craft days, they learn, step by step, to carefully cut and paste coloured paper to create a butterfly, a flower and so on.

In the music lesson, they follow the teacher and play the notes, one by one, on their little keyboards, stopping each time the teacher needs to correct them.

to draw specific shapes like a cat or a tiny box with criss-cross lines that is their house, some will draw a set of connected circles, one on top of the other, that looks like a human being (could be themselves or a family member). Older children of five or six years will draw scenes from their daily life (their house with a tree next to it or their family eating at the dinner table).

On days they have painting, they use a blank sheet that has been soaked in water and a large, wide brush. As they dip their brush into yellow and touch it to their paper, it runs in all directions. The colour is alive and the children are ready to play.

During movement time, the teacher puts on some music and dances along with the children. Children are expected to follow her steps and gestures. Often interwoven in this activity is learning of concepts. For example, through up and down gestures children will be informed about things that go up like a bird or an aeroplane and then also how things that go up also come down, introducing the word gravity to them.	With their brush, they move it, turn it and swirl it around. Meanwhile, the teacher quietly works on her own painting, carefully dipping into the colour and laying it on the paper, using gentle brushstrokes, moving the brush in different directions. She will step in to guide the child only when the child seems like they're done, or their strokes are so hard that the paper starts to disintegrate, or they spill the water on the floor. Meanwhile, a child might exclaim, 'Look, I've made the sun,' and the teacher will nod and acknowledge, 'You have made the sun.'

	With clay, the teacher quietly works on her ball of clay, placing it between his palms and carefully forming and shaping it to make it 'round like the sun'. The children are free to watch the teacher as he works with focus and interest and refrains from offering any instructions or remarks to the children. The children follow his example and use their hands to mould the whole chunk of clay into a ball. Some children will be done at this point. Others would have gone further and created a new shape out of the ball. Singing is present throughout the day, especially during transitions.

The day begins with the teacher leading the children into a morning song in the circle. Children imitate the teacher's singing and gestures and follow along. The music floats into their ears and rises out of their own selves, invigorating their bodies and nourishing their souls. In this celebration of music, there is no place for instruction or correction. As the songs are heard and sung over and over again through the years, children come to appreciate their meaning, recognize it in the world around them and develop a love for music.

Mealtimes	
The teacher announces snack time and the children rush to bring their snack boxes out of their desks or cubbies. Amid loud chatter, the children begin to eat at their desk while the teacher may or may not eat at her own desk. While some children eat their whole snack, many others leave portions in the box. The fallen crumbs are either cleaned up by some staff or left for cleaning at the end of the day. Children wrap up their boxes as soon as the teacher announces that snack time is over. Immediately, they move on to the next activity.	Eating is seen as a sacred time when the world offers itself to nourish and sustain us. The teacher prepares himself to receive this gift and invokes a feeling of reverence in the children for the same. A gentle song sung by the teacher before meal times reminds the children that it is time to eat. Together, the teacher and children lay the table, wear their aprons and visit the washroom to wash their hands. Everyone sits down and the teacher says a verse of gratitude for the food and the children follow along. A quiet calm descends.

	A couple of children assist the teacher in serving the food out of a community bowl. Everyone enjoys the meal in silence.
Story time	
The teacher brings a new story every day to children in the preschool. She sits in her chair, facing the children who are sitting in their chairs as the teacher reads aloud a story from the book. The teacher pauses, turns the book around to show them the illustration of the scene she was just describing.	Story time is the second formal lesson besides circle time. Every day, the children listen to a story from their teacher. The story is not read from a book or shown on a screen; instead, the teacher tells it from her heart. Just before story time, the teacher dims the lights and draws the curtains to a close. She puts on her story scarf or stole and now the children know it's time for the story.

The teacher sits among the children and all come and take their place beside her. She lights the story candle and sings a song to invite the story, in a soft, gentle voice. By now, the children have all calmed down, as they let out a sigh and wait with bated breath for the story to begin. The teacher sounds a gentle melody on a glockenspiel or another soft instrument like a lyre. She plays the same melody each day just before she begins the story. There is absolute silence. The teacher begins to tell a story. She knows it by heart and through its retelling, she has made the story her own.

She then asks them if the picture depicts what she had just read or if there was something missing. The children answer, there is some discussion and the teacher continues to read. She stops the narration again when she arrives at a pause in the story. She asks the children: 'What do you think the cat will do now? Will it give the cheese to the mouse?' A brief discussion follows and the reading continues. Once the story comes to an end, the teacher engages the children in a series of questions and answers based on the story.

She also informs them who an author is and how they are different from an illustrator. The session comes to a close amid much chatter. On another day, the children watch an educational story along with the teacher on the screen. Once the video ends, the teacher initiates a discussion, followed by a round of questions and answers.	The children listen without making a sound. They live in her imagination. It is a beautiful sight: their eyes glaze over and jaw loosens. They are drinking in the story with their whole body. At some point, some might even become horizontal as they slip into the world of the story. At the end, the teacher pauses, breathes and plays the same melody to mark the end of the story. She wraps up her instrument slowly, giving the children time to return from storyland. The story will be repeated every day at the same time for the next three weeks. This repetition creates memory.

	A few days into the story, a child might interrupt and correct the teacher if she forgets to say a word or modifies a sentence. Through this active listening, children are taking in the world through the word and making it their own right down to their bones—a most beautiful inbreath.
Classroom space	
The classroom is brightly lit. The walls are packed with charts of letters and numbers with corresponding pictures, informational posters about animals, plants, days and months, and more, as well as children's artwork.	The lights are softened by a silk veil covering them. The walls are painted using a special technique that lends them a breathing quality.[1] Their pastel pink hues are calming and soothing for the young child.

---

[1] This technique called Lazure involves slowly adding multiple thin coats of colour (ten or more) that give the walls an ever-shifting tone and movement that normally applied opaque paints cannot achieve.

Anywhere the child might look there is something asking for their attention. The space is taken up by brightly coloured plastic desks and chairs. Boxes of colourful plastic toys of all kinds from dolls to blocks and more are kept on shelves along the walls. The seating arrangement with the teacher at her desk, facing the students who are in their own spots, works well for instructing the children, making it hard for the child to access the teacher.	The space draws them in without closing in on them. The walls are devoid of any academic material but might have functional things on them like hooks to hang children's aprons. There is a rug in the play area which is surrounded by shelves containing natural toys and play materials (such as wood, clay, wool and cotton). There is a kitchen where the teachers prepare meals which has a wooden table with small wooden chairs for the children. In the corner is a small table depicting a seasonal scene: a tree made from real branches with soft green fleece for leaves, a crocheted nest

	in which a woolly bird sits on soft woolly eggs to give them warmth, and a little vase with real flowers from the garden to remind children it is springtime. The scene will change when summer arrives. The children do not have designated seats (chairs or desks) and play on the rug or on the floor (when it's warm) and are free to find the teacher when they need her. During story time, the teacher sits among the children on the rug. Some children move closer to the teacher and take their place beside her.

Rest time	
Children move from one activity to another. From chatting in the circle, to reading, writing and math lessons, from games to art lessons, from snacks to stories. Some preschools offer an after-care where children whose parents are working can be cared for. It is during after-school hours that children get some rest time.	Rest time is an essential part of the rhythm during school hours. The teacher dims the lights, and the little ones lie down on their rest rugs. The teacher gently massages their feet and back one by one, humming a soft melody, as the children settle down to rest.
Math	
Children sit at their desks and the teacher asks the children to count the number of children present in the class. Then they name the ones that are absent.	Children are not formally taught math concepts. There are no chalkboards, whiteboards or video presentations. There are no desks and chairs in which children sit, no textbooks

The teacher writes the names of the absentees on the board and the number of students present and absent. She asks the children to read the numbers. Then they are told to read the date written on the board, identifying the numerals in the process. By the time they are five, they are expected to count up to 100, forwards and backwards. The teacher puts additional emphasis on the turnovers in counting, from 29 to 30s, 39 to 40s and so on. Then they repeat it and write it in their notebooks many times over.

or notebooks in which they write, and no worksheets for homework. Instead, they experience numbers through everything they do, especially during circle time, outdoor play, indoor play and chores. They experience numbers through movements and actions. During circle time, they develop one-to-one correspondence as they match their steps to the song or rhythmic verse being spoken by the teacher. When they sell vegetables during free play, they learn, through experience, that two carrots are more than one and ten carrots are much more than one.

Before the end of kindergarten, children are expected to learn addition and subtraction. For this reason, as soon as they learn counting and writing the numbers, children are taught number facts, and the symbols of plus and minus. In some kindergartens, they also learn basic place values. To make them master these concepts, children are given practice worksheets of one- and two-digit operations for homework.	A three-year-old might be carrying three apples to give to her friend; when she drops two by mistake, her friend might point out, 'Oh! You dropped two apples.' When they stack wooden blocks, one on top of another, they unconsciously learn the concept of more and less, 'Put one more,' a child says. 'No, let's put two more. Let's make a really tall tower,' says another. 'No, we must take the top four blocks away or the tower might fall,' says a third. They are also learning about shapes, weight and gravity in the process!

	When they do chores, they develop a sense for sequencing (a prerequisite for counting) through the different steps that must follow one another: before the floor is mopped, it needs to be swept; before we cut carrots, we must wash them, before we bake the dough, we must wait for it to rise.
Reading and Writing	
The teacher points to bold and bright letters on a chart and the children repeat after her as she moves down the chart. A slide show is shown with the big and small letters accompanied by a picture of an object, for instance, 'B' and 'b' along with a picture of a bat.	No formal reading or writing is taught until the age of six. Instead, children bathe in the beauty of the spoken word through circle time and story time. Even during transitions, the teacher uses a song with a gentle melody to guide the children to the next activity.

Seated at their desks, the children copy the letters and words in their notebooks. They practise writing the letters many times over with the help of the teacher's instructions. At some point during this exercise, their shoulders are droopy, they bend over their books, they tilt the book in an attempt to write straight. Some may begin to get shifty in their chairs and lose focus. The teacher corrects them when their letters and words spill over the lines and encourages them to try harder. Practice sheets are sent home with expectations for parents to help the child practise at home.	The entire day is rich with songs, finger rhymes, verses and stories that engage the child through movement and plant the seeds for language development.

Next, they are taught two- and three-letter words. The teacher reads from a book and children read along in their own books, following each word with their finger. In order that the children have a strong grasp on the language by the time they reach Grade 1, they are also taught basic sentence formation, capitalization, simple punctuation and spelling. In some countries, where the population consists of mixed ethnicities, preschools require children to learn three languages. Children are expected to be able to read, write and spell in all three languages before they reach Grade 1.

Which Version Supports a Healthy Rhythm of Growth and Development?

The second version. Here's why:

1. The inbreath opportunities it offers to the child are as close to the natural world as possible and therefore most easily assimilated by the young child for their growth. This includes outdoor time in nature, toys made of natural materials, meals that avoid processed and unnatural ingredients, and circle time and stories about the natural world—like plants and animals and human activities like farming, which are close to nature. A natural environment offers the most immediate opportunity to the child to know the world: It is closest to their own bodies and therefore easiest to engage with through physical activity. Because only the physical aspect can be educated in the early years, these inbreaths constitute the ideal curriculum for a young child's education.

2. The inbreaths in the second preschool are not long, which ensures that the child does not get overstimulated. Additionally, because the majority of the day is full of physical movement with outdoor

and indoor play, circle time and chores, the child is constantly assimilating what they are breathing in. The only pure inbreaths are mealtimes and story times, which are never more than ten to fifteen minutes long. In both cases, an outbreath follows soon after: cleaning up after mealtime and rest after story time.

3. In addition to well-spaced outbreaths, the second preschool takes great care in ensuring that the classroom and outdoor environment protects the child's developing senses. This includes the soft, pastel-coloured, uncluttered walls, use of natural materials and toys in the classroom and playground and, most importantly, the calm, gentle presence of the teacher.

4. Academic teaching that calls upon the thinking capacities (which are asleep in a young child and must not be prematurely awakened) is completely absent in the second preschool. There is no formal teaching of reading, writing and math or use of a teaching style that involves questioning, reasoning and discussing. Also absent is the use of screens or electronic media.

Taking all of the above differences into account, when the child returns home from the first preschool, they have spent the first half of the day largely breathing in the world. Many of these inbreaths are developmentally advanced: instructions, questions, discussions, video presentations, all of which are abstract impressions that the child cannot process physically, which is the only faculty available to them at this age. Even playtime, art and craft activities become lost opportunities when they are structured with rule reminders, questions and conversations. All of these impressions remain undigested. They also sap a child's growth forces by pushing them into the activity of thinking, away from doing. It is like trying to grow fruit on a young tree. When that happens in nature, the tree pays the cost of shallow roots, thin trunk, poor fruit yields and vulnerability to pest attacks.

The two preschools contrasted above reflect two ends of the spectrum. We offer them as benchmarks to assess where your child's preschool falls in the spectrum. Unless it is very close to the second preschool, your child is returning home with an excess of inbreath. It can be hard to have agency over the preschool environment. However, once the child returns home, you are in charge. What can you do as a parent to help your child find balance?

Harmonizing the Child's Rhythm When They Return Home

1. Avoid after-school classes

A young child does not need after-school classes. They are already receiving an intense inbreath during the first half of the day. Adding more to that amounts to overloading a child's senses.

2. Include activities that give the child an outbreath

When your child returns home, create a healthy breathing rhythm for the remainder of the day that replenishes their life forces. Having returned from a long inbreath experience at preschool, the young child needs a nap. This outbreath helps them digest some of what they have taken in during the first half of the day. This can be followed by a snack (a short inbreath), after which the child can engage in another outbreath, say, free play at home with their toys. Free play needs to be at least an hour long, after which the child can wind up their toys. Next, they can help you with a chore. It could be watering the plants, cleaning their cupboard, folding their laundry or chopping vegetables (with a butter knife) for dinner. Now, they are ready for a quick snack before they head out to the neighbourhood park for outdoor play or a hike in nature. This is a much-needed outbreath for the child as they run around and engage in different movements. Observe the child for signs of petering out and start winding up before that happens to head back home. Upon returning home, the child may wash up, put away their bottle and shoes and help in laying the table, which tells them it's time for dinner. Once dinner is done and the child has helped to wind up the table, a bath, followed by bedtime ritual, prepares the child for a sound sleep.

Frequently Asked Questions

1. Should I send my child to a small preschool close to home with few children in a group or a bigger one that is part of a K-5 or larger school?

    Ans: It is best to keep everyday travel to preschool to a minimum as travel is a pure inbreath with overstimulating impressions like traffic lights, noise and the stress of driving. A small preschool with a good teacher–child ratio, 1:6 or less, is a better choice.

2. What factors ought to be considered while choosing a preschool?

   Ans: Choose a preschool that offers:
   - Daily outdoor time, which ideally includes free and unstructured play
   - Indoor time that includes plenty of movement and play
   - Minimum focus on academics
   - Dedicated rest time
   - Warm and loving teachers

3. How many days a week should we send the child to preschool?

   Ans: It is best to begin slowly and allow the child to transition to a greater frequency over time. Start with two days a week for two hours. Gradually, increase the number of days and duration of time once your child has settled in.

4. If one doesn't have the option of keeping their child at home after school, how can one choose a healthy after-school class for the child?

   Ans: Consider these factors when choosing an after-school class:

- Avoid academic classes even when they are brought through games, picture books and manipulatives such as beads, marbles, abacus, flash cards, puzzles and so on.
- Choose a class that involves gross movement (large movements of arms, legs and the torso) and has a playful feel to it. However, avoid formal sports that are heavy on instructions and rules.
- If it's hard to find an unstructured movement class, look for cooking, baking, clay modelling, painting or drawing classes. Choose one that is more playful and less rule based.
- Avoid a class that places the child in a competitive environment.
- Avoid classes that have too many children and feel noisy and chaotic.

5. How many days a week can I send my child for after-school classes?

    Ans: Less is better. Start slow, with once a week for an hour. Only increase to more days if you have no better option. This will avoid over-scheduling. Also, make sure your child is going to no more than one class per day.

6. Should the child go to the same after-school class or is it better to have different classes on different days?

   Ans: Considering that after-school classes are best avoided for a young child, if this is not an option, try and keep the variety to a minimum. Once you find a good class, just stick with it.

7. Which math or creative language class can I send my child to?

   Ans: The young child has had more than enough inbreath at their preschool in the first part of the day. Academic learning is best avoided at this stage of childhood, so an after-school class with academic content is not recommended.

8. Would enrolling my child in a chess class be a good option?

   Ans: Children can be introduced to chess early on by watching adults or older siblings play. If it's in the home environment and the child takes to it, there is no harm in letting them explore. But to coach a child in the game with instructions about rules of the game is an intellectual activity for which the young child is not ready.

The child will be ready for lessons in chess around the age of nine, which is also when grammar is introduced. Learning grammar requires the capacity to understand rules and structure, similar to chess. Children begin to develop causal thinking around the age of twelve, which is when they also begin to grasp strategies of the game with greater awareness and ease. Starting formal training in chess too early will tire the child and they might even lose interest in the game.

9. Is it a good idea to enrol my four-year-old in a ballet or other classical dance class?

    Ans: Classical dance has a strictness of form, which is too limiting for a young child. Their physical body is not yet ready for the strain of repetitive movements because they are still developing muscles and joints (and will continue for several years). The requirement to adhere to form makes the experience intellectual rather than bodily and is tiring for the child.

They can begin proper training around the age of twelve, when their bodies are ready to take on the load of such movements without causing injuries. By now the child has also developed capacities to grasp the techniques with greater awareness.

10. What kind of music class is a good choice for a young child?

Ans: If you choose a music class for your child, look for one that involves singing along with movement and has minimum instructions.

Singing is an instrument of the soul. Young children are in a state of levity, neither fully in the spiritual realm nor on the ground. They are still fitting into their bodies and taking hold of it as their physical being develops. Music is a language they are closest to. Music that is lyrical and melodious and does not have too many earthy grounding notes reaches them, for example, songs in the pentatonic scale. If you need to choose between vocal and instrumental music for a young child, the answer is quite straightforward: vocal music. But here you need to look into what kind of classes these are. Is the child engaged in singing along with the group as they move, hop and skip? This would be the best choice.

A class that focuses on training the vocal chords to strike the right notes and gaining technical knowledge of the notations requires a kind of awareness the young child does not yet have. Such lessons can begin around the age of nine.

11. Is a sport class a good choice for a five-year-old?

Ans: No, organized sport is not for the young child. While the trend these days is to start early, repetitive practice of highly defined movements is not meant for young children. Their bodies are still growing and developing and should not be limited by fixed movements nor burdened with the stress of competitive sports.

- A child who has been playing an organized sport since the age of five or six might lose interest or burn out by the time they're older. 'By age thirteen, statistics show, three of every four children who participated for several years in organized activities have permanently shelved their cleats, Scout uniforms or music books,' says Alvin

Rosenfeld, MD, former head of child psychiatry at Stanford University and author of *The Over-Scheduled Child*.[2]

- Organized sport requires the child to understand the rules and techniques of the game. Young children do not yet have the logical thinking to grasp causality. They may rote learn, but that's a burden on their developing capacities.

This is not to say that a six-year-old cannot play and enjoy basketball, badminton or tennis. But there's a marked difference between play and organized sport. During play, children can stop when they're tired or change the rules to fit their interests and abilities. In a sports class, children must go on to complete the drill as long as the coach demands.

12. Which art class is best for my child?

    Ans: Art is a medium of expression. The more freely the young child can engage with art, the better they will be able to express their inner impressions. Let's look at what is not helpful to a child when they do any kind of art:

---

[2] Nicole Wise and Alvin H. Rosenfeld, *The Over-Scheduled Child: Avoiding the Hyper-Parenting Trap*, St Martin's Griffin, 2001.

- Instruction-based structured activity
- Filling colours in a drawing book with illustrations, forms and shapes
- Focus on technique
- Repetitive practice to gain perfection

When art is brought to a child in the way described above, it defeats the very purpose of art for a young child, which is to provide an outbreath.

Chapter 5

Social Engagements: An Avoidable Inbreath

The human experience is a quintessentially social one. All of our individual capacities, whether physical skills, warm-heartedness or bright ideas ultimately help us connect with other human beings. These experiences, whether positive or negative, carry the potential to move and transform us. They can be as casual as sharing a cup of tea with a friend, or as serious as pitching a business idea at work. On a spiritual level, each time we are with another human being, we are either resolving past karma or creating new karma. Sometimes we can recognize this truth in our lives when we reflect on how a certain decision (a new job, travelling to a new place, picking up a new hobby) led us to meeting someone who became instrumental in our journey. It would not be too far-fetched to say that our life can be summed up by all of the big and small interactions with other human beings.

Given this picture, education and parenting must prepare children to become healthy social beings. While a child develops an independent social life in their twenties, the preparation begins at birth.

Socialization in Early Childhood Is a Physical Experience

In their first seven years of life, children get to know the world through their bodies. This includes getting to know other human beings. The body and the physical senses of life, touch, movement and balance become vehicles for the child's social development. This development takes place in stages. It starts with parents and expands in growing concentric circles over time.

When a baby is born, the mother meets all of its needs and completes the circle of care for the baby. In fact, in traditional societies, babies spend most of their time being carried by their mothers through the practice of babywearing. Close contact with the mother's body not only provides security and warmth to the infant, but also a sense of their own boundaries. As babies become aware of their surroundings, they begin to communicate with gestures and sounds. In the middle of nursing, they pause, stare at the mother and smile their way back to drinking milk. There is eye contact and the first glimmer of human interaction. During the same time, the child gets used to the physical presence of the father through diaper changes, tummy time and bedtime rituals.

Gradually, the child meets more family members and begins to smile, laugh, cry or simply fall asleep at these gatherings. More interactions follow: an uncle throwing them up and catching them mid-air as they giggle, a grandma rocking them on folded knees to the tune of a rhyme, monologues from friends and family, and ambient conversations. The child absorbs these sense impressions all the time: the words, sounds, tones, right down to the emotions, and gains social awareness.

Social development is greatly expanded when children discover the vehicle of speech. The child goes from indistinct babbling to, one fine day, surprising, and even embarrassing, the adults around them as familiar words come pouring out: words and phrases they had been quietly absorbing all this while. This is elementary socialization in which the child unconsciously imitates what is around them.

Around three years of age, the child shifts from referring to themselves in third person to first person, from 'Johnny wants apple,' to 'I want apple.' This is their first experience of individuality, a faint consciousness of being separate, the first of many awakenings in their journey to become individuals. It is also the first step towards acquiring the moral capacity of acknowledging and respecting another human being. They are now ready to play with another child and the circle expands to peers of similar age. This play is again very physical and includes children chasing each other, tumbling about, tugging at each other. It can even include roughhousing, where they unintentionally hurt each other. They might feel surprised and appear clueless when this happens because they never expect their action to cause pain. The next moment they forget about what happened and start playing again. They are discovering their physical boundaries and developing their sense of touch, which will become a cornerstone for developing healthy social boundaries as adults.

This kind of ephemeral play continues for a couple of years until around five years of age, when signs of socializing with more awareness become visible. Five- and six-year-olds can often be found chatting in a corner, planning the next move, strategizing about their play and having conversations. At this stage, the child is able to play comfortably in a larger group of children.

Given this picture of social development, how can parents create the right conditions for their child's socialization?

Developmentally Appropriate (and Inappropriate) Social Engagements

Up to the age of three, home is the ideal space for a child to experience other people and develop from these interactions. After they first awaken to their individual self, around three years of age, they are ready to widen their social circle. Being in their own house or their friend's house or together in a park offers just the right amount of social exposure to the child. When curating the young child's social life, it is best to integrate these engagements into the daily and weekly rhythms. Any abrupt, unplanned engagement throws the child off balance.

The right amount of water helps a plant grow, but too much can stunt it. Loud, crowded settings with bright lights, such as malls, weddings, movie theatres and adventure parks, serve the adult's need for fun, not the child's. Instead, they amount to a huge inbreath, and the child immediately looks for ways to breathe out. They will start running about or spinning around in circles. If they're unable to process the sensory overload through movement, they will start crying to express their discomfort. These behaviours often have a cascading effect, and the child might struggle to eat or sleep afterwards. 'Seeing' your child for who they are is critical to 'meeting them' and fostering their development. The next section answers practical questions on healthy socialization for young children.

Frequently Asked Questions

1. Should a three-year-old miss naptime to meet guests coming over for lunch?

    Ans: No. Having a strong, consistent rhythm of alternating inbreath and outbreath experiences is the key to raising happy and healthy children. Naps and night-time sleep are pure outbreath experiences that allow them to process previous impressions and make space to absorb more impressions. A three-year-old is not yet ready to be a social being in the way older children and adults are. After letting your little one meet the guests, it is okay to excuse them so they can go for their naptime.

It is possible that the first time you try this, your little one resists. But once naptime is done repeatedly, they will come to expect it. They will know that naptime follows lunchtime every day.

2. How should you respond when your child starts having a meltdown in a mall?

   Ans: This can be overwhelming. You try everything, from a carrot to a stick, but nothing seems to work. What can you do? Here are a few tips:
   - If possible, avoid taking them to the mall. Loud, crowded places with bright lights are not meant for a child. A young child's senses are still developing, and such impressions overload the senses.

- Sometimes there is no choice, and you have to bring your child along. In this case, make sure your child has had an outbreath, like a nap or free playtime, before the trip, so they can empty themselves of previous sensory intake before they take in more at the mall. Keep the trip short, half an hour maximum.
- If you are in the middle of a meltdown, don't try to reason with them or to make them understand. Telling the child to calm down also does not help. Keep conversation to a minimum.
- Meanwhile, do not give in to their demands for buying this toy or that ice cream.
- Instead, take them outside, away from the noise and crowd. Hold them in your lap and rub their back as you hum to them.
- Once they calm down, it's best to head straight home where the child can breathe out with a nap or quiet time.

3. Does a four-year-old need to be part of a late-evening wedding because of which their bedtime is delayed?

Ans: No. Weddings are busy spaces with large crowds, conversations, music, i.e., spaces with too many demands on the child's senses. Additionally, when the child's bedtime is delayed, their rhythm is broken. Protect your young child from such social settings and prioritize their rhythm when it is a matter of choosing one over the other.

4. How to set up the first play dates for your little one?

Ans: As your young one takes their first step outside their inner circle to socialize with peers, remember to do it gradually, in a rhythmic manner.

- Start around three years of age.
- Fix a time on one day of the week with one friend.
- Stick to the same friend for the first several play dates.
- Meet outside in a park or any other open, natural space so that the children can get to know each other and not be distracted by their toys or other things at home.
- Do not guide their interaction. They will play by themselves as they roll in the dirt or make tunnels in the sand. They will climb up the ladder and

slide down, share laughs and falls. If they need you, they will come to you.

5. How often should your child have play dates?

    Ans: To begin with, have once-a-week play dates and fix the day and time of the week. Keep this rhythm for a few weeks until your child gets adjusted to them. Then fix a second day of the week and allow your child to go through the same adjustment. Once your child is around four years of age, you can expand their circle to include a second playmate.

    Overtime, the three children can come together on play dates and the frequency and group size can increase gradually as long as it is consciously added to their rhythm and adhered to consistently.

6. How long should a play date be?

    - For children below three years, a play date should be no longer than an hour or so.
    - Three- and four-year-olds can do well playing with other children for one to two hours.
    - Children who are five and older can play for up to three hours.

- To prevent them from spinning out from too much play and physical movement, break for a snack in between.
- Start and end play dates on time, so that the rest of the day can proceed according to their usual rhythm.

7. Your two-year-old is playing with her stuffed toy and your friend's child wants the same toy and starts to pull at it. How can you respond?

   Ans: The first thing is to do nothing and simply observe because things usually resolve on their own. Either the other child will find something else to play with or your child will leave their toy and start playing with something else.

   If one of the children starts to cry, they need to be comforted. Go close to them and gently rub their back and arms. Hum a gentle melody. Pick them up and put them in your lap. This will calm them down. Then place another toy in front of them to give them another possibility of play.

Remember that:

- Such young children are not capable of sharing because they don't experience themselves as separate from their environment. Because they feel one with both the toy and the other child, they don't see a need to share.
- Don't feel a moral burden to make them share; your child is not being ill-mannered or mean.
- Also, little children do not have the emotional or mental capacity to consider their friend's desire for the toy and honour it. So, telling them how the friend is feeling will not help. Offering logical reasons is also premature for this age.
- They are constantly curious about their surroundings and are not attached to one thing for long. So, they will move to the next toy before you know it.

8. What to do when your four-year-old refuses to share their doll with another child?

   Ans: Around the age of three, the child starts to feel separate from their friend. The child may not be easily enthused by bringing another toy in their sight. They will hold on to their doll while the other child continues to tug at it. What can adults do in this situation, especially if one or both children begin to cry?

- Humming a tune and a gentle rub will help calm them down.
- What will not help is talking to them. Any logical conversation or instruction does not reach the young child. So, telling the child to say sorry or, 'Your friend is feeling hurt' will not help, as they do not have the emotional capacity to comprehend another's feelings.
- Remember they are in the 'doing' phase. Make a little story about a doll who needs to feed her cat. This image will engage them and soon enough both children will flow into the image and come together to help the doll feed the cat.
- Once both children have calmed down, speak on behalf of the second child to the first one. 'Johnny says he wants to play with the doll.' Then speak on behalf of the first child. 'Mia says she is ready to play once her doll has fed the cat, who is very hungry.' This way you have acknowledged each

child. You can now round off by saying, 'The cat is done eating and both Johnny and Mia are ready to play together.' Give a gentle rub on their backs and send them off to play.

Chapter 6

How Parents Impact the Rhythm of Growth

Parents are the centre of their child's world, not just because they take care of all their needs but simply by virtue of who they are. Even as the child widens their environment to include a nanny, grandparents, a neighbour's child or preschool, the parent remains most immediate to the child. No picture of the rhythm is complete without the parent.

It is clear that screen use, school, after-school classes and social engagements are inbreaths that the child has to work hard to digest. What about their first environment? The parent. What impressions do parents bring to a child? Let's find out.

Parent as Inbreath

The most obvious way in which children show us that they absorb impressions from their parents is when they start imitating them. What about impressions they breathe in but cannot digest through imitation? Let us look at both.

1. Parent's Actions

Because young children's way of interacting with the world is through their physical body, a parent's actions and gestures are most readily taken in, even when they are not directed at the child. Their processing also begins as soon as the child finds the freedom to play and act them out. The simpler the action, the more easily the child can assimilate it, like beating imaginary eggs in a bowl, walking around with folded arms or slamming the door when leaving a room. A child will refuse to eat carrots if he has never seen his parents eat them but will happily ask for chips and fries if that's a common sight around him. The most ubiquitous impression available to a young child today is parental screen use.

2. Talking with Children

Parents begin to talk with their little ones as soon as they are born, and often prior to that. Whether the infant is gazing into the distance or smiling or crying in response, it feels satisfying to the parent to connect in this way. When babies grow a little older and are able to say their first words, it is a joyous milestone and the talk becomes more intentional, often involving naming things for them. At some point, around two or three years, the monologues turn into first conversations between the parent and the child. From the child's perspective, the words and sentences that flow their way are an inbreath. When they are spoken without a physical context, such as an object, an action, or a sensation, they are pure information, which a young child struggles to digest. How does this affect the body's rhythm of growth? Does the type of conversation matter? Let's take a look at the most common conversations between parents and their little ones.

Instructions

Parents are often telling children to do something. Because a child is in a 'doing' phase during the first seven years, they have not yet developed the capability to listen to an instruction and translate it into action. Every parent knows this to be true. An instruction is abstract; it doesn't have a physical existence that they can imitate.

It is no surprise then, that instructions fall on deaf ears when not accompanied by actions. When this happens, parents go into survival mode and start using every trick in the book. 'Come on, let's prepare the salad together. It will be so much fun and it will taste delicious!' 'You must eat healthy food. Fruits are good for you, otherwise you won't grow tall.' 'Go and put your shoes in the rack, or it will make me very angry.' 'Come, let's do this worksheet. Then you can watch TV for some time.' The excitement and enticement, the fear and guilt, the reward and coercion might work now and then, but, for the child, they create insecurity, the need for external gratification, and an expectation to be entertained in order to accomplish something. In the long run, this lopsided reliance on emotion-driven instructions weakens the child's sense of life and their will forces.

Meanwhile, whether the task is completed or not, the instruction still has to be digested by the child like any other inbreath. If they're lucky and have dedicated play time, they might be found telling their doll to put its shoes in the rack. If we think of all the instructions given to a child from morning to night, we quickly realize how they sap the parent's and child's energy without positive responses from the child or building of healthy habits.

Giving information to children

As children start to become aware of their environment, they notice more and more things. A two-year-old points to an insect and screams with great excitement, 'Look, what a big ant!' A three-year-old shouts 'ice cream' as an ice cream cart passes by. A four-year-old says, 'Look at that big moon!' These are moments of pure delight. Little snapshots of the growth that is going on inside them. The parent's heart swells with pride and joy. Out of enthusiasm, they start a conversation. 'Ah! I see. But you know, it's not a big ant. It's a baby butterfly. It's called a caterpillar. After a few weeks, when it eats and grows, it will turn into a butterfly. Then it will fly away.'

Questions are even more exciting. 'What is that?' a little one asks pointing to a ladybug. 'Where does the sun go at night?' 'Why are the birds singing?' 'Why do you have to work?' As they grow older, around five or six years old, the questions change. 'Where has Grandpa gone and will he come back?' 'As himself or someone else?' 'When will you die?'

As adults around the child, we feel obligated to provide the correct answer. We try to explain the concept of rotation and revolution or the mystery of life and death. But if we are really observing, we will notice that we lose the four-year-old's attention halfway through our first sentence!

Let us deconstruct what happened. The child shared something that caught their attention, and the adult took it as a cue to educate the child. Not a big deal on the face of it and fairly natural too. But was the child really seeking information? Were they looking for answers or simply wondering aloud? Is the information meeting the child's need or the parent's?

When this happens repeatedly, the child is prematurely pushed into thinking, and it halts their process of wonder, inquiry and making sense of the world at their own pace. Giving them logical reasoning in these early years is like throwing rocks in their gentle stream of imagination. They also struggle to persist with a question because they have developed a habit of getting an answer right away.

Looking at the span of a whole day, the inbreaths add up. What is a child to do with them? They cannot imitate information. If they're given a chance to play, they might say the same things to a doll or a friend. Otherwise, the inbreaths pile up, waiting to be exhaled.

The other thing that happens when children receive a lot of talk from adults is that they are forced into speech sooner. These are children who stand and talk rather than move around and do things. There's nothing terrible about standing and talking per se. However, it is not the task of a young child and takes the place of their true task. The child is catapulted to a later stage of development before they have finished the task of early childhood. The child's inner forces are diverted away from moving and forming their physical body and senses towards speaking and thinking. They are having an experience of ingesting words about the world rather than knowing the world through their bodies. This is a missed development. If this continues, children develop a certain nervousness about them; they retreat a bit unto themselves rather than staying open and trusting to the world, a thinning of their sense of life.

Baby talk

On the other extreme is baby talk. In those moments of pure bliss, when your baby looks into your eyes, breaks into a smile and chuckles, your heart melts into a puddle and out come all sorts of made-up words, words you didn't know existed. Gibberish for milk, for sleep, for food, for their favourite toy—all desperate, sloppy expressions of the flood of love you feel in your heart. (Those utterly sweet and incomprehensible nicknames are often born in these moments.) As you carry on with your sweet drivel, your baby delights at the sound of your voice and responds with more cuteness and so it goes.

Until it gets old. Your baby soon outgrows the baby talk, but you carry on. The baby starts speaking their first full words, being cuter than ever, and you invent more gibberish to convey your overflowing love.

So, what does this have to do with inbreath? Well, the gibberish is an inbreath. But a poor one. It is like giving baby food to a child who is ready to chomp on solids. Remember that it is through breathing in the impressions around them that the child grows and learns as a physical being. But baby talk gives them little to work with. So, it is no surprise that as they learn to talk, out pours the same gibberish! Meanwhile, the opportunity for learning real language is missed.

Asking children questions

When a parent is with their child, questions are never far behind. 'What did you do at school today?' A fairly reasonable question at pick-up, you would think. Not for a young child. The inner experience for a child is that of being stunned. They are suddenly asked to dive into their memories, identify the ones related to school that day and convert them into an answer for the parent. Children do not even begin to retain memories until they are four and it takes all of adolescence for memory development to be completed. But because the parent is expecting an answer, the child is forced to think of something.

Questions push the child into thinking. But the young child has not developed this capacity yet, so they might say 'Nothing' or 'We played'. The answer the parent gets is clearly not informational, defeating the original purpose. And it could be worse. The child might say something erroneous, like something that happened a couple of days ago, or something they heard in a story or overheard an adult saying. This does not mean that the child is lying. It simply means that when pushed to recall, they offer the last most impressionable experience. This is totally natural for the young child, but the outcome for the parent could be confusion or even worry. In the end, it is wasted time—an unnecessary inbreath for the child and stress for the parent. The child was asked to do something they were not developmentally ready for, and the result was unsatisfactory. Like looking for sweetness in an unripe fruit.

Asking children to make decisions

More and more parents are breaking away from the traditional, top-down parenting they received from their parents. They want to be more inclusive and involve their child in making decisions concerning them. From decisions regarding the choice of preschool ('Did you like it? Do you want to go to this school?') to everyday matters ('Do you want to wear the red dress or the blue one for the birthday party?') to food choices ('Do you want to eat fried eggs or boiled eggs?') When the child says they don't want eggs, the parent strategizes about how to bring it to them with another question, 'Can I make you a pancake?'

Let's look at what is happening for the child. At the most conscious level, the child is again pushed into thinking and that too of the highest order—making judgements. The faculty of judgement is not fully formed even in teenagers so asking young children for their preferences is misplaced.

At a deeper level, such questions throw the child off. 'My parents don't know' is the unconscious response that arises. Because they cannot quite comprehend, it leaves them feeling unsettled. For the young child who sees the world as good, asking them to choose creates an inner disturbance. They are being asked to go against their natural gesture of oneness to compartmentalize good and bad. But because there is an expectation of an answer, the child, out of their love for the parent, obliges. With time, this becomes a pattern, an acquired habit. By the time they are four or five, they frequently declare, 'I want to wear the blue dress,' or 'I do not like carrots. I won't eat them.' Now, the parent is taken aback. *Why has my child become so fussy?* they wonder. A struggle over every little thing in daily life ensues. Meanwhile, the child's inner forces are yanked away from the task of physical development towards premature thinking.

3. Ambient Behaviour

While parents' direct interactions with children are clearly impactful, their behaviour, even when not directed at the child, is just as important. Remember that a young child is constantly soaking up impressions, so a heated conversation happening around them or something serious taking place in the family is just as much an inbreath for the child. When they cannot imitate the words because they are too new, they will pick up the tone and pitch. During play, you might find one doll (parent) crying because the other (grandparent) is very ill and dying. For the young child, death is not a painful occurrence the way it is for an adult. Children do not have the emotional capacity to feel sad in the way adults do at the prospect of losing someone. But once they receive the impression, they need to digest it.

The same is true for intangible aspects, such as thoughts and emotions. If you are anxious, your child will exhibit signs of restlessness. This is why when you have a late-evening plan to finish pending work or go out for a social gathering, your child will not fall asleep easily. Nothing looks different on the outside; you are following the regular routine with them and yet the child senses your restlessness.

If you are parenting from a place of anger (even when not directed at the child), it will unsettle the child. If you are exhausted, it will show up in your child's behaviour. Some children will manifest it by withdrawing and becoming quiet. Others will become clingy, demanding more attention, and getting angry when they do not receive it. Overall, the child will need to process this sensory load from the parent.

Parent as Outbreath

When the time spent with you allows your child to digest previous sensory impressions, you are an outbreath for them. When does this happen in a day? Every time you give them the opportunity to play and move about freely. Every time you cuddle with them. Every time you roughhouse with them, play tag and chase them around. Every time you sing and dance together. Every time you take them out into nature or garden with them. Every time you rest together.

How to Be a Balanced Parent for Your Child?

If becoming a parent has turned your life upside down and turned you inside out, you are spot on. You simply cannot remain the same person once you've become a parent. You are now responsible for guiding the path of a new human. It's time for growth.

Growth means change, and changing things about yourself is uncomfortable. A few things can help. Remembering who the young child is, their need for rhythm and that who you are affects this rhythm. Second, to choose to grow out of freedom rather than compulsion. Finally, reminding yourself that the longest journey begins with one step.

1. Step one: breathe out

Who are you when you are around your little one? Calm as a lake or torrential like a waterfall. Are your thoughts and emotions well-integrated or are they often brimming over? Are you regularly digesting what you are breathing in, or do you have unresolved inner matters that tend to linger and make surprise appearances when you are with your child?

Before you can be fully present for your child, empty yourself.

As adults, we take on multiple roles both in professional and personal lives. And somewhere in the rush of life and the many hats we wear, we forget ourselves. We forget to take care of ourselves. We forget to breathe. *Can I take the afternoon off from work and just relax at home or go to a spa?* Immediately, a list of to-dos pops in our head. *If I pause now, I'll fall behind at work. If I take the afternoon off, shouldn't I spend it with my child?* When we talk about creating a breathing rhythm for the child, we have to remember that it cannot happen without parents creating one for themselves first.

So, what are the first steps you can take to breathe out? Start where you are.

- If you're driving to pick up your child, to work or to run an errand, sing your favourite song. Put on songs that reflect your mood at the time and sing along.
- Before you go to the kitchen to get dinner ready, put on a face mask. By the time you're done, the mask will be too, and you will start dinner feeling refreshed.
- When you go for a bath, take thirty seconds and put a few drops of essential oil to the water. If you don't have a tub, do this for a footbath.
- When you go to bed at night, spend a few minutes journaling about the day.
- If you play a sport or have a fitness routine, do not miss it. Prioritize it by finding care for your child.

- When you start dinner, take a moment to light a candle. Just looking at the flame can bring us to a place of rest. This can be a time of giving gratitude. Hold hands and, if you feel inspired, say a prayer.

As you begin to create these spaces of reprieve, your day will feel more balanced.

To take this a step further, create new islands of outbreath:

- Start the day with nature. Spend a few minutes gazing at the sky or the trees outside your window, or if that is not possible, water your plants. Spend time with them. Run your fingers through the leaves, feel their texture and notice the veins.
- Take a few minutes at any time of the day, whether at home or at work, to sit down and have a cup of tea without your phone or laptop. Think of one thing you are grateful for and say it out loud.
- Find ten minutes to walk after dinner or early morning.
- Include a ten-minute workout, which can be five simple stretches.

- Take a few minutes to dip your feet in warm salt water at the end of the day.
- Take up an art that you're drawn to. You don't need to be an artist to do art, but by doing it, you will naturally breathe out. If you can find a class that helps you release rather than train you, take it up. If not, start at home. Buy some paints or clay and play with them. If you like to dance, put on music and dance away.

The most important thing is to start where you are, with one act of breathing out, and to do it consistently. Whether you commit to doing it every day, every week or every month, once you start, stick to it. As you build this rhythm for yourself, the rhythm will carry you.

When you come into a more balanced state and your little one sees that you care for yourself, while caring for them with enthusiasm, not exhaustion, they will carry this learning into their life as adults.

Now that you have brought harmony into your day, you will bring more balance into your interactions with your child.

2. Avoid being an inbreath for your child

- Make decisions for your child, big and small.
- Lead the child by doing, not by instructions. For all the daily tasks a child needs to accomplish, like brushing their teeth, eating their meals, putting on their clothes, putting their toys away and more, lead the child by example. When the parent picks up the toothbrush and starts brushing their teeth, the child will readily follow with their own little toothbrush.
- Step into wonder with your child.

  When a child asks, 'Why is the moon so big today?' remind yourself that your child is not looking for an answer. They are simply marvelling at the beauty of the world, much like a poet. You can acknowledge with a nod and simply repeat, 'I wonder why the moon is so big today.' And take a moment to truly wonder about the moon. Meanwhile, let the child stay with the question, so they can arrive at explanations in their own time.

- Bring consciousness into conversations around the child.

  Avoid disagreements or discussions about a serious matter when the child is around. The young child's organism is not developed to accommodate thoughts and emotions. If you need to talk over a disagreement or discuss a serious family or work matter, wait till the child is no longer in your vicinity.

  The same is true if you wish to discuss the child themself: 'Which school should we choose for her?' 'You know how naughty she has become! Today she ate her friend's lunch.' Or make pure value judgements like, 'She has become stubborn', 'He is such a simple, helpful boy' or 'She is so intelligent'. As children get to be around five or six and start understanding the meaning of abstract words, they take in these words and start believing them. This is an undesirable consequence because fixing one idea about themselves can get in the way of them truly getting to know themselves and grow into self-aware individuals. So, talk about your child when they are not around.

- Bring consciousness to language
  The young child is learning to speak. Whether they hear beautiful songs or cuss words, they will repeat it. If you don't want your child to speak poor language, avoid speaking it around them.

Similarly, don't dumb down your language for them. Young children need to be spoken to in full, coherent sentences using appropriate words. This is how they gain language skills.

Chapter 7

Eating: The Most Important Inbreath

How often do we think about eating? That which creates us as physical beings and sustains us in the world. Eating rarely occupies our attention, hardly even receives our time. We eat on the go, while crossing a street, driving a car, catching an elevator, attending a conference call or watching our favourite show. Eating is slapped on, like mortar between bricks, habitually, even mindlessly, its critical role of holding life forgotten.

Traditionally, eating has always been a time of coming together to receive food with reverence and gratitude. Prayers before meals are common across cultures and religions. In Native American tribes, food is not just something you put in the mouth. It is the story of a people, with every food carrying a myth or legend, often about its origin. Food is not simply grown or bought, but ceremoniously planted, harvested, gathered and hunted. Prayers and songs accompany its preparation and consumption. On the other side of the world, in the Bhagavad Gita, the Hindu god Krishna reveals himself as the supreme cosmic spirit that pervades and enlivens all creation, even the act of digestion: 'Acting as the fire of digestion, I, entering the body of every living entity, digest the four types of food by the auspices of the incoming and outgoing life breath.' (The Bhagavad Gita, 15:14)

Eating: The First Crucial Inbreath

In our fast-paced lives, eating has lost its primordial meaning. So, when we become parents, we are hardly prepared to bring the child into a harmonious relationship with food. What is this relationship?

At birth, the baby takes their first breath, and life begins. Not long after, the baby needs to take in their first food. Doctors recommend that a baby be put to the mother's breast (or alternatively fed) within an hour of birth; the sooner, the better. Eating, then, is an essential inbreath experience. Through eating, the child partakes a little piece of the material world and makes it their own. The substances of the world work their way into the child's organism which digests and assimilates them. This assimilation manifests as growth, and little by little, with every feeding, the tiny human being grows and becomes a part of the world.

Eating Has to Be Learned

Learning to eat is a huge endeavour on the part of the child. A baby must learn to breastfeed, to latch on correctly, to suck with enough strength so they can get enough milk. A strenuous task, it requires all of the child's life forces, evident from the way the infant is exhausted by the end and falls asleep at the breast, sometimes even before they are done nursing. Nursing is such an intense inbreath that only the deepest outbreath, sleep, can digest it. As babies grow and gain more strength, they are able to nurse for longer durations. Now they don't need to sleep to recover. They simply pull away when done, ready to play. Babies who start with formula have a steeper climb, breathing in sensory experiences like the taste and texture of formula and the bottle nipple, both more foreign than nursing.

And that's just the first six months of a child's life. Next comes solid food—a whole new task that engages the child's physical senses more strongly as they take in complex tastes, textures, smells and colours. The child has to get to know the food in order to make it their own. As Albert Soesman, a doctor and educator, says, 'First we have to have a serious, quiet, though forceful, conversation, which means eating patiently, chewing well, making an effort. The tongue assists and guards the process. We have to add moisture, and work it over ... by tasting you have to ascertain that the food is compatible with (your body).'[1] For the child's sense of taste to develop well, we need to start slowly, and gradually introduce new tastes, beginning with bland, semi solid foods, then adding salt and moving to solid foods, followed by introducing simple herbs and spices, and so on. When the child has the opportunity to progress in this way, the metabolic system can learn to do its work, and the sense of taste can develop at a healthy pace without being overloaded with variety. It also teaches the child to sense when a certain taste feels good and when it does not.

And so it continues. With every new food, the child is on a new curve: eating, digesting, assimilating and discarding, and in the process, learning about a little piece

---

[1] Albert Soesman, *Our Twelve Senses: Wellsprings of the Soul*, Hawthorn Press, Stroud, Gloucestershire,1998.

of the world. Eating grows the child, educates the child about the world and prepares them to eat more, a constantly expanding inbreath.

Eating is a material conversation we have with the world. A child comes into the world naturally eager to have this conversation. But it is not a given that they will be able to. Eating requires two preconditions: (1) the child is not distracted by other 'conversations' and (2) the child has emptied themselves of the contents of previous 'conversations'.

Too Many Sensory Impressions Distract the Child from Eating

Remember that a young child is constantly soaking up sensory impressions around them. And not just with their eyes or ears, but with their whole body. Their body is one, singular sense organ. A nursing baby expresses contentment by moving his arms and legs. A toddler expresses their joy at hearing their parent's voice by running, jumping up and down, and flailing their arms, all at once. Strong impressions have a more striking impact. A child sucking on a lemon feels its sharpness in their whole body, compared to an adult who might only contort their mouth.

When the inbreaths are developmentally appropriate, the child assimilates them easily and is ready to take in more. But if a child is in an environment with a lot going on, their body is quite literally unavailable to take in the most important sensory impression—food. Unlike adults, young children cannot ignore bright lights or loud noises and still be able to eat a full meal. A baby will keep turning their head towards another adult in the room and only be able to eat once the adult leaves or when the mother physically turns the baby's head towards the breast or bottle. As they get older, intense mealtime conversations and screen use can get in the way of the child eating with all their senses and establishing a connection with the food.

Previous, Undigested Inbreaths Prevent the Child from Eating

Children also struggle to eat when they are still carrying undigested impressions from before. A three-year-old who has just returned home from a long drive in traffic will be slow to transition to mealtime. A four-year-old who is called for dinner right after they've been watching something will struggle to sit down and eat. Often, in these situations, the child will run around the house or roll about on the floor. They are trying to balance themselves, to breathe out the intense impressions they have absorbed before they can be ready for the next inbreath—eating. If they are made to sit down at the table, they might say, 'No, I don't like soup,' and start banging their spoon on the table. Usually, in these situations, the parent turns to the screen for help. But does the screen help the child converse with food? Or does it distract the child enough so that the parent can feed the child, and the child eats passively without engaging all of their senses?

When parents are faced with challenges related to eating on a frequent basis, a common response is to offer the young child more choices. The child says, 'I don't want soup' and because the parent dreads the oncoming meltdown or because they are tired and out of patience, they offer the child an alternative. 'Shall I make you your favourite pasta?' The child nods in agreement and the parent lets out a sigh of relief. But because the sensory overload is undigested, the child remains in a near-constant state of stimulation and food tantrums continue to happen. Eventually, parents run out of alternatives and children get labelled as picky eaters.[2]

---

[2] In rare cases, children can seriously struggle with the smell, taste and texture of certain foods, typically due to an underlying medical condition or previous trauma. These children especially benefit from reducing the sensory overload and may need medical help as well.

When parents resort to a quick fix, it might temporarily make the child eat but never truly enable the child to connect with food. As a result, the experience of fully relishing each bite, looking forward to the next one with anticipation, and finally, reaching a point of satiation fails to happen. This is a missed opportunity for development because it becomes hard for children to develop a sense of life, the sense that informs them of well-being in their body.

What Can Parents Do to Help?

Because eating itself is the most fundamental inbreath a child needs in order to survive and grow, and because it takes continuous learning on part of the child, be careful about the other inbreaths in your child's rhythm. Remove or reduce intense inbreaths such as screen use, homework, social engagements and make time for outbreath experiences like play, movement and sleep.

Next, create a mealtime ritual for your family.

- Fix the time for meals.
- Place an outbreath activity such as a trip to the neighbourhood playground before mealtime that helps the child process previous inbreaths.

- Add an anchor such as washing hands and setting the table that tells the child that mealtime is approaching and they can transition to it easily.
- Say a prayer before the meal or some words of gratitude if you're not religious.
- Eat with the child. Make sure that you are eating the same food as what the child has on their plate. Do this every time, even if you have dinner plans later.
- Model healthy eating habits for your child to emulate. Sometimes, the impressions preventing the child from eating the food in front of them come directly from parents. When a parent says, 'Don't put broccoli on her plate. She doesn't like it.' the child will repeat the same and say, 'I don't like broccoli.' This is just the young child imitating the adult, but the parent takes it at face value and stops giving broccoli to the child, effectively establishing that they don't eat broccoli. When a parent says, 'I am not hungry now. I'll eat later' and snacks on a bag of chips, or if they pick

out carrots from their plate, the child is likely to follow suit.
- Keep conversations to a minimum, and eat with your full attention.
- Afterwards, clear the table together with the child.

Frequently Asked Questions

1. Why are mealtimes such a struggle with my five-year-old?

   Ans: Use this stepwise checklist to identify the reason:
   - Your child is snacking in between meals and is not hungry at mealtime.
   - Your child is constipated.
   - Your child is not getting enough exercise and movement during the day to build a healthy appetite.
   - Mealtime gets delayed and they get tired and sleepy.
   - Your child is not sleeping enough or sleeping poorly. This reduces their appetite and makes mealtimes a struggle.
   - Your child has a sensory overload from the day's inbreaths and cannot wind down to be able to eat.

- There's healthy food on the table and they're in the habit of eating junk food. They do not have a connection with healthy food, so they have no interest in eating it.

2. Why do I struggle to make my child sit during dinner?

   Ans: Movement is the natural state for young children. They experience their environment by moving. This is how they learn about the world and themselves. This is also how they grow. To expect them to sit at a table continuously for an extended time is premature. This is not to say it is okay for them to be running around forever, but it will take them time to learn to sit for the whole duration of dinner.

   So, if your child runs around during mealtimes, here are some things you can do:

   - Make sure the child has had an outbreath before coming to eat.
   - Create a calm environment, without loud noise, conversations or screen.
   - Keep mealtimes from getting too long. Fifteen to twenty minutes is a good length to aim for.

- If they run away, don't run after them. Let them come back to you.
- Always include finger foods which they can eat easily on their own and develop a sensory relationship with food.
- Initially, a little distraction will help them transition from running around during meals to sitting in one place. The best way to do this is to tell them a story (not read from a picture book) where the 'rabbit hops to the burrow to nibble on the carrot'.
- Gradually increase the time in the story when the 'rabbit' is eating. Now, it stays in the burrow to eat the whole carrot before hopping away again.

3. My child takes too long to eat and gets late for school? What should I do?

Ans: Remember that eating is something the child has to learn. Eating takes time and the child must be given this time. Review your child's daily rhythm, especially bedtime, to make sure they're sleeping early to be able to wake up fresh so that they have thirty to forty minutes to eat before leaving for school.

4. Why is my child so fussy about food?

   Ans: A young child does not inherently have likes and dislikes the way adults do. For most children, when they say they like something or hate something, it is learned behaviour. That means they have either:

   - heard someone say it and are simply repeating it,
   - or they have been asked whether they like something or not and they have had to come up with an answer.

Over time, it becomes a habit for the child.

5. Should you offer alternative options to your children if they are fussy eaters?

   Ans: No. Here's why:

   - Having to decide is a burden on a young child.
   - They have not developed independent likes/dislikes yet, so when they're given choices and asked to decide, they push themselves to do it because their parents are expecting an answer.

They are unable to say 'I don't know.' They are too young for that.
- Having to choose causes them discomfort and makes them fussy. 'No, I don't want strawberries. I want guava.' You bring them a guava and they don't eat it. They want an orange now, and so it continues.

So, do not offer alternative options to your child.

6. How can I help my child eat everything?

   Ans: Here are some changes you can make to help your child eat what they're offered:
   - Avoid passing value judgements like good, yummy, tasty, yukky about food—whether it is food you're eating, they're eating or someone else is eating. Even if you have likes and dislikes about food, it's best to keep them to yourself. You want to leave your child free to form their own likes and dislikes as they grow older.
   - Avoid asking questions like, 'You like beans right? They're tasty!' Again, you're asking them for a value judgement. They're too young for it.
   - Model healthy eating habits that the child can imitate. Avoid eating junk around your child.

- Cultivate their interest in foods they fuss about by inviting their imagination. Tell them a simple story like: 'When I was little, one day I was eating carrots and a rabbit came hopping and sat in front of me. The rabbit was hungry, so I gave it my carrot and with its tiny teeth it nibbled away.' You can pick a carrot and start to nibble at it. Your child will imitate you and start eating the carrot.

- To help them transition to eating items they are not in the habit of eating, bring it to them as finger foods. You do not need to create a fancy presentation to get them to eat. This is a slippery slope as the child will develop a habit of expecting a fancier presentation every time. Food by its own nature is inviting to the child when they have a healthy appetite.

- Engage them in preparing the meal and laying the table. This way, they become a part of what they are about to eat. They will not avoid the food they have worked so hard to prepare.

- Eat together with them even if you only take small portions and take joy in it. You are modelling

a healthy relationship with food and they will imitate it.
- Avoid screen time while eating. This distracts them and becomes a hurdle in developing a connection to the food.
- Avoid offering alternatives if they are not eating what's on the table.
- Let them go to bed hungry. This sounds radical, even cruel and will be the hardest to do. But every once in a while, if they're fussing at the dinner table and refusing to eat, gently say 'It's okay.' The food will now go to rest and the kitchen will go to sleep. It will come back when you wake up in the morning.' Then carry on with the next thing in the rhythm.

Remember that weaning your child off a habit takes time. The key is to keep at it and over time they will start eating more foods.

7. My child doesn't eat vegetables. What can I do to help?
   Ans: Your child needs to form a connection with vegetables. Here are some ways to create this connection:
   - Visit a farm and let your child participate in the activities. Make sure you do this a bunch of

times and not just once. It is best if you visit the farm at sowing and harvesting times every year. Consistency is key.

- If you don't have a farm near you, help your child grow some vegetables at home. When the time comes, harvest them and include them in your meals.
- Engage your child in preparing the meal. Let them help you wash vegetables, peel boiled potatoes, shell peas and tear greens for a salad. As they get older, give them a butter knife so they can chop vegetables like carrots and cucumbers.
- Take them vegetable shopping with you. If you usually order online, make sure to find time at least once a week to buy from your neighbourhood grocer.

8. Is my child eating enough?

Ans: Here are three ways to tell:

- Your child is active throughout the day and sleeps well during the night.
- They have regular bowel movements.
- Your child is growing in height and weight.

9. How can I wean my child away from the screen at mealtimes?

    Ans: Just like forming a habit takes time, so does unlearning it. You will need to be patient, persistent and consistent. Here are some steps to make mealtimes screen free:

    - Walk the talk! Make sure you do not watch something while eating. Children imitate us so be mindful of what habits you are modelling to them.
    - When trying to wean your child away from the screen, simply put all the screens to 'rest'. This is a boundary you will need to hold with love even in the face of tantrums and tears.
    - Remember that 'telling' them to turn off the iPad will not help. Be cautious of offering your young child any explanation or logic to avoid negotiations.
    - Along with taking away the screen, you will need to bring something in to fill the gap as you transition your child to screen-free mealtimes. Engage the child with a story or anecdotes from your childhood. The child is used to being distracted while eating. This will offer a healthy

alternative to the screen in the process of weaning them off. Gradually, they will learn to eat without the need to be distracted.

- Eat along with your child so they have a reference for imitation.

10. Is it important that we eat together with our child at mealtimes?

Ans: Once your child begins to eat solid food, they should eat the same food as you together at mealtimes. Here are three reasons why this is so important for the child:

- Children learn by imitation and mealtimes are perfect for modelling good behaviour to your child. They will watch you sit and eat, and they will try to do that themselves. They will want to eat the food you're eating. They will take joy in it when they see you enjoying the food. They will learn so many things just by watching you do it: how to eat different types of food, how to combine foods into a more satisfying bite, how to use cutlery and so on.
- Meals are a time to bond as a family. By coming together and sharing a meal, you renew your

connections as a family. Warmth is created that the child experiences and feels safe and secure in it. Avoid difficult topics and electronic devices at the table. It is a special time. Keep it that way.

- Meals are a perfect time to give thanks as a family. To express gratitude for the food and the opportunity to eat together. Too often we are running from one thing to another and eating on the run. By creating space for mealtimes, we acknowledge the sacred act of sharing a meal and the child receives this value for life.

Chapter 8

Play: When Children Naturally Harmonize Inbreath and Outbreath

Play. How does the word make you feel? Light. Joyful. Relaxed perhaps. Close your eyes and repeat the word. What do you see? Children running around, laughing, busy doing things. The word 'play' comes from the Old English word 'plega', meaning to move lightly and quickly, and the Middle Dutch word 'pleien', meaning to leap for joy. It also comes from 'plegojanan', meaning to occupy oneself or take charge of. When we talk about the play of children, it is all of the above. It is hard to find children who are playing and not moving, playing and not appearing light and joyful, and playing and not occupying themselves and taking charge.

'Play Is the Work of the Child'

Attributed variously to Italian physician and educator Maria Montessori and Swiss psychologist Jean Piaget, this quote sums up the place of play in a young child's life. When a child is not sleeping or tired, or being directed by an adult, they are busy at work and this work is play. Delighted by their surroundings, they engage with them. The engagement brings more delight, spurring more engagement and more delight. This is the young child at play, a spontaneous immersion into the world around them born from instinctive interest.

During play a child is 'reading' the world. Their openness fills them with wonder about everything, whether it's a broom or a doorknob, a stick or a stuffie. Drawn by their sense impressions, they wander from object to object, eager to know each one. Everything is a 'book' waiting to be 'read'. The only difference is that this reading is not just done through their eyes. They use their arms and legs, hands and fingers, feet and toes, nose and mouth, eyes and ears. This is most easily seen during meals, when eating: children often play with food, covering their whole body with it. Play in early childhood is a whole-body experience.

Play is also when a child 'writes' their story. This 'writing' also happens through the whole body, a physical processing of what they've been 'reading'. The teacher or parent who has had the good fortune of observing a young child at play will have seen this beautiful and significant digestion at work. The child is playing out all they have taken in from the world, whether it is something that happened at home that morning or events from the previous day, several days or even months ago.

The 'writing' can be of all kinds: a house full of guests with the child busy preparing tea and snacks to serve, a big doll singing a lullaby to make a little doll sleep, a mother shopping for groceries, even a traffic accident with cop cars blaring sirens. As the child plays out these impressions from the world, they get assimilated, and the physical body learns and grows out of it.

> A four-year-old child in Ukti's kindergarten returned from Summer break with a peculiar behaviour. He would all of a sudden run behind other children making sounds of a dragon breathing fire. He was fearful and

alert, always looking over his shoulder. During story time, he would cling to the teacher. Discussions with the parents revealed that the child had been listening to a story about an angry dragon who blew fire at a whole village and destroyed it. The story had made a deep impact on the child. It is only when he returned to the kindergarten, where an hour-long play time was a consistent part of the rhythm, was he able to process this undigested inbreath.

Play then is the highest form of education. It is self-education. Through play, a child makes sense of the world. A child who has been allowed to play in childhood is capable of educating themselves throughout life. This capacity for teaching themselves is a shining flame that can light their path, no matter how thorny. And that's not all. Play raises a human being to their highest potential.

> If a child has been able in his play to give up his whole loving being to the world around him, he will be able, in the serious tasks of later life, to devote himself with confidence and power to the service of the world.
>
> —Rudolf Steiner

A child who plays thoroughly and perseveringly, until physical fatigue forbids, will be a determined adult, capable of self-sacrifice both for his own welfare and that of others.

—Friedrich Fröbel

Implicit in these quotes is the assumption of freedom. A child who is given the space and time to play out of their own self, receives the most precious gift childhood has to offer. This freedom to play bestows health on the child and confidence to follow one's path as an adult. When children play on their own, they alternate between inbreath and outbreath based on their individual needs. Some children will be mostly busy acting out the impressions they've received from their environment (outbreath), while others might spend more time taking in impressions (inbreath) and each will go back and forth based on what their bodies need. During play, the child's organism freely chooses its rhythm of growth. Play enables the child to self-regulate and find harmony within themselves. Play strengthens their sense of life.

Play: An Endangered Experience

Fifteen years ago, kindergartens in the US were found to be in crisis. 'Children (were spending up to) six times as much time in literacy and math instruction as in free play . . . teachers (were) spending (up to) 30 minutes per day preparing kindergarten children to take standardized tests.'[1] This distortion of education, squeezing play out of children's lives, was happening at the same time as 'leaders of major business corporations (were) saying that creativity and play are the future of the U.S. economy'[2]. Today, these misplaced expectations have been passed down to preschools, and children as young as three are being encouraged to recognize letters and numbers. The situation in the rest of the world is not much different. With the pressure of academic expectations spilling over to home life, play has all but vanished out of childhood.

It is no surprise then that the United Nations observed the first-ever International Day of Play, on 11 June 2024, in an effort to 'preserve, promote, and prioritize playing so that all people, especially children, can reap the rewards and thrive to their full potential'.[3] More generally, there has been a mushrooming of play-based preschools and

---

[1] *Crisis in The Kindergarten*, p. 11. Why Children Need to Play in School. Edward Miller and Joan Almon. 2009.
[2] Ibid.
[3] 'Play Makes a Better World', https://www.un.org/en/observances/international-day-of-play (accessed 17 February 2025).

kindergartens around the world which promise free play and the use of playful methods of instruction. It is not clear how well this language translates to reality. The very fact that play is now always accompanied by the adjective 'free' tells us that the word has lost its original meaning of light, joyful, self-directed activity.

As educators, we witnessed firsthand the disappearance of play among children. When children first joined Ukti, very few knew how to play, that is to alternate freely between inbreath and outbreath. The calm environment of the kindergarten, with its soft colours and gentle sounds, gave children a break from being stimulated. This pause allowed children to release pent-up, undigested impressions from previous inbreaths that had not found the space and time to be processed. Some children moved around constantly, speaking content from adult conversations or T.V. shows. Others made noises of all kinds. A five-year-old made loud digging noises and gestures (imitating a digging machine from a show he'd been watching). This went on for weeks as he ran around, moving like the machine, oblivious to what other children were doing. Another five-year-old spent all his time outside, digging in the sand pit. After doing this every day for three weeks, he came up to the teacher and said, 'Where is my class? Where are my friends?' As soon as he entered the classroom, he ran to the play corner and joined other children in their play. All of these children were emptying themselves of previous unassimilated experiences.

Until children are able to exhale such impressions, they feel restless, disturb others and even show unexpected aggression like screaming, pushing and hitting. Their first brush with freedom allows them to release their previous impressions. It takes them time to feel comfortable with themselves and feel a sense of well-being, before they can initiate play. The teacher often has to lead them in the beginning, 'Look, that horse is hungry. Take this bowl and fetch some food from the kitchen.' Images like this help to ease them into play, until they are able to do it by themselves.

What Can Parents Do to Help?

Parents have the greatest agency to make play an integral part of their child's life. The first thing is to educate themselves about the importance of play. Then create the space and time for it. Give children the right inputs for play, like open-ended toys and art materials, as well as rich stories. Practise self-awareness and avoid questions, comments and conversations with the child while they are playing. And, finally, make time for outdoor and nature play. Here's how to begin.

1. Understand and honour play

Because play happens organically and often slowly, while our modern world functions with speed and efficiency, play is the first thing to get thrown out to make space for things that seem more important to an adult mind. But a child's need for play never ceases. It only changes in form. It is important that parents recognize these forms so they can appreciate and honour them as key developmental and educational milestones during their child's early years.

Bodily play. Children begin to play from the time they are infants. Their first toys are their own hands and feet. As they grow and begin to move around on all fours, they begin to interact with their environment and find things to play with. Bowls and spoons that they can access, mud and sand, and anything else that is in close proximity. Because the world is good for the young child, everything around them is worthy of becoming their toy. Toddlers who have gained a vertical view of the world find a whole new dimension to play with. A pen on the table can be picked up and opened and closed, a bowl on the kitchen counter can be grabbed and rolled about on the floor, the T.V. remote can be reached and the buttons pressed endlessly. The child will repeat these actions till they know them well. However, their attention span is short and they will gravitate to the next thing that makes a sensory impression. At this stage, children play by themselves, largely unaware of another child playing in the same room (parallel play). Their play is not social in this sense.

Imitation play. By the time they turn three and the first consciousness of their self is born, they begin to become aware of other people and things around them. If they have seen a parent host a tea party, they might host one during play in the kitchen corner or use a block as a phone and hold it between their ear and shoulder, just like their parent does. They will build a tower that is their apartment building. They may tell their doll, 'Eat the banana.' A ladle may become a gun they aim at others and shoot like they have seen on a TV show. The fact that a ladle can become something else during a child's play is their fantasy at work. Their dreamy consciousness easily straddles the real and the fantastical. As the child grows older, this early experience of play paves the way for imagination to develop.

Planned social play. Play goes through yet another shift around the age of five. Now you will find children standing in a group in a corner, chatting about something that happened. Sometime later, it will find its way into their play. They assign roles: 'You be the policeman and I will be the driver.' They spend some time discussing the props: 'Let's use this cardboard box to make a car.' They are actively putting their imagination to work. If the 'car' falls apart, they will reconvene as a group to figure out a solution. Perhaps they need to use some glue to hold it together. With this intentional quality entering play, it can be remembered for longer periods and returned to the following day just like a work in progress. They might request the parent to let their car be in its place until they play again.

When children are given ample opportunities to play freely in their early years, they build capacities for excelling in their professional and personal lives, like taking initiative, working as a team, problem-solving, out-of-the-box thinking, and executive function skills: mental processes that enable us to plan, focus attention, remember instructions and juggle multiple tasks successfully.

2. Create the space and time for daily play

Just like you have locked in your child's mealtimes and bedtime (or have been trying to!), block off time for play. Children need at least two hours for play after they return home (three to four hours for children four and older). The younger the child, the more crucial it is for this block of play to be interspersed by multiple inbreaths. Five-to-fifteen-minute snack breaks are the perfect inbreath. As children get older, fewer snack breaks may be needed.

If your child struggles to enter into play, which may be the case when they are overstimulated, they will need your support to start. To support indoor play, begin by eliminating any overstimulating impressions in the home environment like loud music, adults on the phone or watching television, especially during this time. You may, for instance, put a cloth on the television or unplug it and let your little child know that the television is resting. With five- or six-year-olds you may need a more clever solution. In any case, the screen must be inaccessible to create an opening for play.

At first, the child might struggle and not know what to do with themselves. They might throw a tantrum if they are used to regular screen time. Let them go through this discomfort. Hold them, care for them, but do not give in. If they retreat to a corner and sulk, it is okay. After some time, they will get bored and come out. Once the stimuli from the environment are eliminated, they will become interested in their surroundings and start finding things to play with.

3. Offer Materials for Spurring Play

The child will play with what is around them and accessible to them. What they play with will transform them. All motor and sensory activity during play forms the physical body and the physical senses. This is a prime parenting moment. What can you offer them for play?

<u>Toys: A little goes a long way</u>

Because young children have a relationship of oneness with everything, and because they experience the world as good, they will play with everything they encounter. But are all things in their environment equally good for play? Every parent knows how nerve racking it can be to childproof the house. We even cushion furniture corners to eliminate any possibility of injury. We do not want any harm to come in our baby's way. But what about aspects of their environment that offer little possibility of growth? During the time in their life when they are most actively growing, is this not a kind of harm? Does an iPad offer the same potential for play as a set of wooden blocks? With both present in the environment, and the iPad offering far greater stimulation to the child, the child will gravitate towards the iPad. Can we leave it up to the child to choose the best toy for themselves?

How well a child uses their play time for healthy growth and development depends on the play potential of their toys. Toys need to be a gentle inbreath as well as provide an avenue for breathing out. If the toy is too stimulating, it will crowd out the possibility of digesting previous inbreaths. Which toys offer such a vast scope? The simplest ones. How can a child use a pop-up educational toy that sings the alphabet at the press of a button to process what happened at school that day? How can a princess doll complete with accessories transform into a mother, teacher or neighbour? The child responds by discarding such toys after a few uses.

Parents take this behaviour to mean that the child is bored and buy them new toys. Soon, the child begins to ask for more toys themselves. The toys start to fill the shelves and take over the cupboards. They spill into the living room and bedroom, then into the bathroom, kitchen and car.

The child continues to flit from one toy to the next, struggling to play with any one for long. And the parent

Play

begins to worry. *Does my child have a short attention span? Do they have difficulty focusing?* Meanwhile, the child's need for a toy remains unfulfilled.

On the other hand, simple materials like cloths of varying lengths and natural textures (cotton, silk, wool), wooden blocks, and cloth or wooden dolls with little to no facial features can represent a wide range of impressions. The cloth can be a meadow, river, roof, cape and more. The blocks can turn into a bridge, a tower, the child's house, a castle and whatever else the child needs it to be. A simple doll can become any human being during play, even a person on the street.

> It is far better if you make a doll out of a linen rag than if you give the child one of those perfect dolls, possibly with highly coloured cheeks and smartly dressed ... What are you doing if you give the child such a doll? You are preventing the unfolding of the child's own soul activity. Every time a completely finished object catches its eye, the child has to suppress an innate desire for soul activity, the unfolding of a wonderfully delicate, awakening fantasy.

You thus separate children from life, because you hold them back from their own inner activity.

—Rudolf Steiner
(The Child's Changing Consciousness)[4]

Isn't it amazing that a few items can cover all of your child's play needs? But there's more. The simple stuff doesn't get old. A set of wooden blocks, especially with varying shapes, textures and sizes, will continue to engage the child over time. As a two-year-old, they will simply pick and place the blocks and repeat this over and over again, in between sucking and chewing on them. As a three-year-old, they will begin to stack these one on top of the other and marvel at the fall of the tower they have built, only to build it again. As four-year-olds, they will build houses and buildings, bridges and tunnels with these blocks, as their experiences widen. As five-year-olds, with greater control over their motor skills and a new-found ability to plan their play, they might start building an airport and tell the adult to leave their creation so that they can come back to expand it the

---

[4] 'The Child's Changing Consciousness and Waldorf Education GA 306', The Rudolf Steiner Archive, https://rsarchive.org/Lectures/GA306/English/RSP1988/19230418p01.html

next day. The blocks grow with the child to represent more complex pictures of the world. The child is also learning to be inventive in their play because the toys are not ready-made but have to be created by the child, afresh every time.

The absence of ready-made toys fosters collaboration and social skills around the age of five. When they build a house in the sand and want to water the 'garden' in which they have sown 'seeds' but do not have a hose or a bucket, they will come together and dig a trench for the water to flow to the 'garden' from the faucet—an introductory experience in engineering, problem-solving and teamwork.

The final word of praise for open-ended play materials is their gentleness and patience. They wait quietly to be discovered and employed by the child. They don't use bright colours, flashy lights or catchy sounds to entice the child. Because such play materials are not demanding a child's attention, they allow the child to have an immersive, even meditative experience during play. This is a pure exhalation compared to highly defined and sophisticated toys that dump more impressions on the child and end up being an inbreath themselves! With open-ended toys, parents can finally create child-led play rather than toy-led chaos.

Art materials

The same is true for art materials. A set of thick crayons (for ease of holding by little hands) and blank paper, a slate and chalk, and some playdough or clay, can meet a child's artistic needs throughout the early years. Their simplicity allows the child to process all kinds of inbreaths. Unlike a tracing pad or drawing book, blank paper leaves a child free to express what's living in them rather than fit a certain shape or form. Unlike an electronic drawing pad, crayons allow a child to see the correspondence between the colour of the crayon and the colour they bring on paper—an experience that rings true to their senses. Unlike drawing pads, blank paper lets the child have an outbreath rather than be fed with images and information—an intrusive inbreath. And finally, nothing can surpass natural clay or playdough in the range of expressions and tactile processing.

Telling stories

Throughout their first seven years, a child continues to absorb impressions from their environment that they need to process and assimilate, and play offers the highest possibility for this task. At some point, typically around three years, their daily environment is no longer enough to learn and grow. They need more. This need is met by stories. Because stories take from the real world and yet have an element of fantasy, they meet the young child's dreamy consciousness. They help the child make sense of the world. Stories are an intentional inbreath that offers an educational experience to the child. And play time provides the stage in which children act out and digest these stories.

The younger the child, the simpler the stories need to be. The best stories are those that are based on everyday life, close to physical reality, something that the child can relate to through their senses: the rat scurries around and hides under the table as the cat watches, waiting to pounce as soon as it comes out. Stories about a little duckling who lives with her mama duck and papa duck are just the kind of expansion a child can relate to. Parents can bring stories from their own childhood, connecting the child to the past, of how life used to be, their first lesson in history: 'When I was a young boy, my friends and I used to play soccer for hours in the evening until dark.' Story about a little girl who lives in a faraway land, where it snows every winter and the trees become bare with icicles hanging from the branches serves as a first lesson in geography. Repetition stories are wonderful for young children as they help strengthen the memory that has just started to develop. 'The little girl who was flying the kite called her brother to hold the string, but the kite kept flying up, up and away. Then the brother called a friend to help hold the string because the kite went flying up, up and away. Now the little girl, her brother and the brother's friend were holding the string, but the kite went flying up, up and away. The friend called his uncle to hold the string . . .' For the young child, stories need to be simply narrated, devoid of emotional nuances or characters that represent a polarity of good and bad. Because the young child's experience of the world is good, stories need to mirror that.

As the child grows, around the age of five, the stories can become slightly longer, with more details, for instance, the tailor who had a big moustache and a long white beard and so on. Simple fairy tales like 'Sweet Porridge', again devoid of polarities in character and nuanced emotions, can be brought at this stage. Children act out these stories when they have an opportunity to play, which helps them develop capacities for imagination and memory and make sense of their expanding world.

Stories serve another purpose. For children who are overstimulated and struggle to play, they provide an entry point to process undigested impressions during play time. For example, a child who has heard a story about Mama Bear, Papa Bear and Baby Bear will now have access to these characters to play out an experience from their home life. For instance, Baby Bear replies to Mama Bear, 'No, I want the sweet honey,' when Mama Bear brings him a bowl of rice and says, 'You must eat rice. You have had too many sweets. This will make you strong and big.' Once they have entered the world of play through a story, children begin to assimilate not just the story but everyday experiences as well.

The best stories are those that are told face-to-face and heart-to-heart. The intimate connection between the storyteller and the child allows the child to enter into the story. When the child hears the story, an inner need for creating mental images arises, developing the faculty of imagination. This process is interrupted when the child is being read to from a book, especially a picture book.

4. Step out of the way

A young child is one with the world around them. This is the case during play as well. When a child is at play, they are completely immersed in it and experience no separateness. They are the farmer, shopkeeper, princess, traffic cop and more, depending on which aspect of their world they are digesting and learning that day.

Imagine a scene where a child is building something with blocks. An adult sees the rising stack and asks, 'Wow, that's a tall building! It is beautiful. How many floors does your building have? Come let's count together, one, two, three...' As a grown-up, if someone were to notice our work of creation and take interest by asking questions or offering appreciative comments, we would be happy to oblige with a prompt response and feel gratified. But if we were really engrossed in something, it would feel disruptive. What a young child experiences when an adult comments or asks questions about their play is no different. They were not expecting any feedback nor asking for appreciation, so any interruption by an adult is simply that—an interruption.

During play, the child works out their sensory impressions and nascent memories through bodily actions. The scenes they create during play unfold one after the other in a sequence of impressions and memories. Any conversation jolts them out of their world, halts the digestion and learning that is in process and pushes them into conscious thinking. Their primary developmental task is stopped, and they are asked to do something that is not yet born, thinking. Their first response is usually silence, because the comments and questions are foreign to how they relate to play. Words of appreciation are empty and fall on deaf ears as far as the young child is concerned, for they are in the stage of 'doing'. For them, gratification and reward lie in the completion of the task at hand, which, in this case, is to stack the blocks to create something.

But if urged repeatedly, the child will oblige. Over time, the child will learn this behaviour and start seeking the adult's appreciation. They will play for the adult, not for themself. This is a tragic outcome: an infringement of the child's freedom.

So, what can the adult do while the child is at play? Sit on the side (at some distance from where the child is playing) with an awareness of the child's safety, and work on something that requires physical activity. This could be cutting vegetables, cooking, sewing, mending, cleaning or gardening, to name a few. Working on your laptop or being on a conference call in the vicinity of a child who is at play will not work because the child might be drawn away from their play. On the other hand, when the child sees you working physically, they will be able to imitate your motor movements and quality of attention and bring these into their own play.

5. Visit a neighbourhood park

While indoor play is a necessary reality because of our largely indoor lifestyles, being outside offers far greater possibility for movement, which is essential for the child to inhabit their physical body. So, include a trip to your neighbourhood park in the daily rhythm, where your child can run, skip, climb, crawl, swing, go up and down a slide, roll on the grass, play in the sand, and engage in rough-and-tumble play. Free play in an open, outdoor space allows for the healthy development of gross motor skills and the twin senses of movement and balance. Children develop spatial awareness, and their movements become more coordinated. They know how far to throw the ball to make it land where they want. Every time they walk on a log or run down a slide, they develop their sense of balance, a foundation for auditory learning and for being able to sit at a desk.

6. Take your child to play in nature

Nature offers the widest range of impressions to develop the child's physical senses without overstimulating them. For instance, when they trip over a rock and fall on muddy ground, crawl or run barefoot on grass, and dip their toes in a cold stream, it awakens their sense of touch, and over time, such encounters bring an awareness about the boundary of their own physical body vis-a-vis the world. The varied textures a child can explore in nature tell them that it hurts when they brush against a thorny bush which feels different from the soft touch of flower petals. In the dry season, grass can poke the soles of their feet, while in the rainy season, it feels soft and gentle. When they play in the dry sand, it slips out of their hands even as they try to hold on to it, while wet sand allows them to create many things. The sound of rustling leaves and gushing waters, chirping birds and crickets, the croaking of frogs, all serve to develop the child's sense of hearing. The sight of a grey sky giving way to a rainbow or the rising and setting of the sun offer the necessary variety for a child to develop the sense of sight. The patterns and colours of a butterfly, the different colours of flowers in a garden and the changing colours of leaves on trees as seasons change offer a breadth of sensory inputs that cannot be replicated by other means. Climbing a tree strengthens their sense of balance and swinging from its branch their sense of movement. The feeling of wet earth under their feet as they navigate a muddy path, the smell of wet earth when it has just rained, the touch of raindrops falling on their skin are tactile, sensory experiences that are true and serve to gently awaken and develop the senses.

Nature does not attract attention to itself, and when it does (say bird calls), it does so in the gentlest ways. So, in nature, a child is able to release any unprocessed inbreaths they are carrying in themselves. Digging in the sand, making mud balls, splashing in a stream, sliding down a snowy hill, climbing up a dirt hill with loose rocks, and more, allow the body to exhale completely through the fullest range of movement.

Nature offers infinite possibilities of play no matter how old the child. On the muddy banks of a creek, a baby will sit and look around, following the gliding motion of a dragonfly with his gaze; a toddler will develop tactile skills as she sculpts mud into messy balls using her palms; and a six-year-old will arrange sticks and stones to engineer a dam to stop the water flow. A child who is anxious or stressed might simply sit by the creek and watch it flow. After a while, when they are feeling calmer, they might stretch their hand to touch the water. One tree can offer something to every child. You can play hide-and-seek around the trunk, climb on to a branch and sit on it, swing from it or hang upside down, play with leaves and notice the veins, craft a boat with leaves and twigs. Because nature does not direct or control, the child has the freedom to create their own play. If one creek or one tree can offer so many types of play, imagine the endless possibilities of being in the woods, in a vast meadow with tall grasses or on a sandy beach by the shore.

Nature never gets old. Every time a child revisits a spot, it has something new to offer. As children grow older, they start to notice the smallest of changes from the last time they visited: an unexpected yet excellent way to hone their powers of observation, a necessary precursor to STEM skills of problem-solving, critical thinking, creativity and logical reasoning.

Finally, what can compare with the pure joy one experiences in nature—an unexpected call of a bird to its mate, the rustling of trees in the breeze, a lizard scurrying away to hide under a rock or a turtle basking in the sun. A joyful child is immediately interested and curious about what happens next. This is the beginning of all true learning. And nature offers it simply and without a fuss. A child who receives this gift of learning directly from nature is one who connects deeply with the world and feels at home in it. The child trusts the world and feels confident of their place in it—a key building block of social–emotional well-being.

For the first time ever in human history, we are experiencing the greatest disconnection from our natural surroundings. The fact that from a health and well-being perspective, we hear more and more that we need to 'spend more time in nature' quickly reveals how we spend most of our time: at our desks, in front of screens, in automobiles and on couches. 'Nature is not only nice to have, but it's a have-to-have for physical health and cognitive functioning,' points out Richard Louv, who coined the term 'Nature-Deficit Disorder' in 2005. Today, his point of view is backed by over 1000 research studies. For children, spending time in nature is not just beneficial, it is critical.

When nature stops being a part of our life, it becomes a stranger. As with anything that we don't know, fears of all kinds creep in. When we encounter it, we tread with caution and mistrust. As adults around a young child, we invariably pass on these emotions to our children even when we don't verbalize them. It is no wonder then that for many children today, dirt is bad and splashing in puddles is messy. 'Don't climb the tree, you'll fall and get hurt,' 'Don't go out to play right now, it's raining,' 'It is too hot today to play outdoors, you will fall ill.' Over time, children start to imitate this fear and aversion of nature, which prevents them from engaging with it. A young child is inherently attuned to nature until the adult world mediates and gradually disrupts this connection. Dark, closed spaces, lit with artificial lights and full of human and gadget or device sounds, spaces requiring little to no movement, have replaced children's play in nature. But childhood play is incomplete without it.

What Must Parents Avoid to Encourage Play?

The answer is simple: screen time. Regular screen use is a direct threat to children's play. Children will struggle to engage with open-ended toys if they are regular consumers of screen images. Because those images are highly specific and get fixed in a child's mind, the child will be hindered from seeing a knitted doll as a representation of a princess. They will also struggle to form images from the stories they are listening to because they are saturated with far more powerful screen images, with the result that the purpose of stories to be a rich input for play is lost. Finally, children with regular screen use will be reluctant to engage with real sensory experiences in nature because they are used to being stimulated by screen content. They will not know what to do with themselves in nature and complain about boredom.

Play is disappearing from childhood and no one is ringing the alarm bells. This is a real crisis and parents are the only true stakeholders who can meet it. The good news is that even a small step towards including daily play in the child's rhythm can help. The child, with their natural inclination for play, will lead the rest of the way. You simply have to clear the path.

Chapter 9

Home Chores: A Highly Effective Outbreath

As adults, we do many tasks in a day. Apart from work, there is an endless list of things to be done at home. The thought of chores is usually unpleasant, even stressful. After all, who likes routine stuff? Sometimes, we manage to outsource them and that feels like a little triumph. Unlike adults, children have a vastly different relationship to chores—a playful one. In return, chores help children develop healthy bodies, take initiative and see a task through, prepare for academic learning, and care for and respect their environment.

Chores Are a Natural Step in a Child's Exploration and Learning

A young child, for whom it is natural to be moving around the house rather than sitting in one place, seeing an adult cut vegetables or fold laundry is an extension of their own natural state. Out of their innate tendency, they are drawn towards the activity and start imitating it. From the child's perspective, this is no different than play. That becomes apparent soon enough when they fold one item of clothing and hop away the next moment, returning to fold another one a bit later. This is a complete breathing cycle. They breathe in an impression from their environment (adult folding clothes) and then proceed to do it themselves, an outbreath. Through each such experience, the child assimilates yet another part of the world around them. Overtime, as they participate in chores, they gain a bodily understanding of a work process and build a physical memory of it. When they wear the T-shirt the next day, they remember that they had folded it.

Chores Provide a Powerful Outbreath

Any physical task involves movement, which allows for the processing of impressions. While a child begins by breathing in the adult's actions of performing the chore, it is quickly followed by the child imitating those same actions, i.e., an outbreath. In fact, as long as this process avoids verbal instructions by the adult, doing chores is largely an outbreath. And it gets better. For a child who is carrying undigested impressions, daily chores offer a reliable vehicle for processing them. As educators, we have often seen this with new children entering kindergarten: for example, a child who got interested in mopping the floor with a wet rag and could not seem to stop. As he moved the rag from left to right, he pressed down on the rag with all his might, applying far greater force than needed. The parent was then advised to drop him fifteen minutes before school started, so he could have the extra time to mop and breathe out pent-up impressions.

Chores Prepare the Child to Be a Learner and a Doer

The purposeful aspect of chores makes the child feel that they are partaking in real work. Father brings the groceries, Mother prepares the food, child lays the table and the family comes together to eat. A beautiful inner realization arises for the child. Through my actions I make things happen. By engaging in a process from start to finish, children gain a physical understanding of the effort it requires. For instance, if they have to water plants, they need to fetch the watering can, fill it with water, water the plants and put the can away after they are done. If they spill the water, they need to wipe the floor. Chores teach children about the magic of human effort. When we work on our surroundings, we make them better. We have what it takes to transform things around us: raw flour into dough, a seed into a vegetable and a vegetable into soup. When they begin, the dough might stick to their hands, the plant might get overwatered and the vegetable chopped into irregular pieces. As they struggle through the process and keep coming back to it, the result becomes better over time. Having such repeated experiences strengthens the will of the young child. This is a reward in itself and the child will not need incentives to begin a task or appreciation to continue it. The child will grow up knowing that they can do anything they intend to and are not wary of working through challenges. This inner confidence carries them through their learning journey both as children and, later in life, as adults.

Chores Are a Foundation for Academic Learning

At its simplest, having chores in the daily rhythm develops the child's capacity to learn sequentially. The many steps involved in baking bread must happen in a certain order to produce bread at the end. When the child routinely engages in such processes from start to finish, they gain a physical sense of sequence which becomes the basis for learning letters and numbers. In fact, this sense is the foundation for acquiring new skills, problem-solving and organization.

The movements and actions required to do chores also create physiological changes in the child's body that lay the foundation for academic learning. Most chores involve a crossing movement from the left side of the body to the right and vice versa. For example, when wiping the table after dinner, the child will initially use small motions but, as they imitate the adult, they will start moving their arm from left to right and back. This vertical midline crossing strengthens the connection of neural pathways between the left and right brain, which spurs cognitive development and the ability to grasp academic concepts.

Today, this important developmental step is missed by more and more children because they simply do not move enough, let alone do chores. A telltale symptom is when a child rotates a paper 90 degrees to avoid writing horizontally from left to right or when they use two separate circles to make the figure eight instead of one continuous crossing motion. This deficit also hampers their success with reading, causing them to lose their place in the text, jump lines, and end up with red, watery eyes. Because they cannot move smoothly from left to right, they continuously shift their body in their seat to the left or right side of the paper. This struggle with the body develops into a struggle with higher-order thinking, an ability to evaluate and make judgements. A simple example in elementary school is solving a word problem in math and in higher classes to form a judgement on an article or find connections between two texts.

Chores Foster Reverence

In our kindergarten, there was a four-year-old who was kneading dough to make bread. Halfway through the task, she took a deep breath and exhaled, 'Wow! This is hard work!' Another time, while having soup that the children had worked hard to prepare by cutting the vegetables, a little boy exclaimed, 'Look, my carrot!' pointing to a piece of carrot floating on top. Because they experience hard work and push through to finish the task, they know better than to waste even a crumb of bread or the last spoonful of soup. They appreciate what they receive because they have a connection to it. They learn that bread doesn't magically appear at the table nor laundry in their cupboard. With time, they understand and appreciate all the good things in their life and the people who make it possible, whether it is the chauffeur, the house help, the guard at their preschool, their nanny or their parents. A quiet feeling of reverence for the world and its people grows inside them. This feeling metamorphoses into a genuine interest in the world in their adolescent years.

The Invisibility of Chores in Modern Life

Not very long ago (and even today, in many parts of the world), home chores were a mainstay of daily life. Young children were home in their early years and naturally participated in chores as the day's rhythm unfolded, from little ones shelling peas with their grandma to older ones peeling and chopping vegetables. Each child engaged themselves every now and then in different chores that were led by adult members of the family. Through learning by doing, the child started to assume independent responsibilities by the time they reached puberty.

Today, most home chores are mechanized or outsourced and rarely visible to the child. Plus, the child is not home in the first half of the day to witness them. The one or two chores a child witnesses when they return home are hard for them to imitate because they happen in a time-bound efficiency mode. For example, dinner is being cooked in the shortest time possible, whether by the parent or house help, and this rushed pace leaves little room for a young child's playful participation. As far as the child is concerned, it is a shrinkage of their learning environment and a missed outbreath. This is poignant because this shrinkage has happened in parallel with intense inbreaths filling up their day (screen time, school, after-school classes and adult social engagements).

What Can Parents Do to Help?

Once the child returns home, dedicate some time when you are engaged in a physical chore and the child is free to watch you do it. It needs to be something the child can try and over time learn to do. For children around three, this need be no more than fifteen minutes. By six or seven years, it can increase to thirty to forty-five minutes. Keep the same time every day. This will help both you and your child stick to it. Here's how to go about it.

1. Reverence for the task

Have you felt a deep appreciation towards a tomato as you were cutting it for salad? As you felt its smooth skin and beautiful colour, did you feel grateful your family will receive this gift from nature? As it mingled with the other vegetables in the salad, did all the colours bring delight to your heart? In forming this connection to the task, did it not feel lighter, even enjoyable?

It is not often in our daily life that we immerse ourselves with such joy in a task. This is even more so for chores because of their mundane nature.

When creating an opportunity for children to engage in chores, however, it is important for you to bring intention to the task, an intention to fully attend to what you're doing. This will make you interested in the task, and this quality will naturally draw your child in. As they follow along, they will be able to imitate the same gesture.

When this quality of presence is absent in the adult, the child can easily be left out. As Rahima Baldwin Dancy, a lifelong early childhood educator and professional midwife, shares:

'Once I was throwing a cake together in a great hurry. I told my four-year-old she could help, but I was going so fast I wasn't paying much attention to her. Suddenly I noticed something was wrong. "What's the matter?" I asked. "You're stirring it too fast!" she said through her tears.'[1]

2. Reverence for the child

Setting an intention to give all your attention to the chore will also prepare you to receive the child with reverence. It will help you remember that what is known and easy for

---

[1] Rahima Baldwin Dancy, *You Are Your Child's First Teacher: Encouraging Your Child's Natural Development from Birth to Age Six*, 3rd ed., 2012.

you, to the point of being boring, is new and full of wonder for the child. In the seemingly simple act of folding clothes, they are bringing the entirety of their being to bear upon it. When they finish folding a shirt, they have made their imprint on the world and on themselves. What you just witnessed will fill you with deep respect for their effort.

It is crucial that you allow their actions to unfold organically and not correct them or redo their work. Instead, keep modelling for them your intentional gestures as you complete the task. Your gestures will be taken up by them and, over time, get better.

3. Consistency is the golden key

To make chores a part of your child's life, do them consistently. Singing a simple melody to start the chore is tremendously helpful. The young child who is closer to the spiritual world and has only begun to be an earthly being resonates far more with music than with verbal instructions. So, make up a song for the chore. The rhythm of the song will carry you and your child through the task with ease and joy. This is not unlike the practice of songs accompanying traditional farming activities of sowing and harvesting, threshing and winnowing as bodies moved to the rhythms of the work. The same is true for the young child as they meet the world with their body. Over time, the child will form an association between the chore and the song and will even begin it before you do.

Frequently Asked Questions

1. Which chores are best for a young child?

   Ans: Children as young as two or three years old can start with chores that involve gross motor movements, for instance, sweeping with a broom, dusting furniture, washing clothes, scrubbing dirty surfaces and watering plants. You could also include chores like arranging clothes in the cupboard or laying the table. These chores should be continued well into elementary years, after which children should be given independent responsibility for them. In addition, as the child gets older, fine motor chores should be added. Starting around four years, kneading dough to make bread and squeezing lemons to make lemonade are good additions. They are also wonderful sensory experiences as the child will invariably want to touch and taste the ingredients. The next step is to peel, shell and chop different vegetables and fruits. And finally, around the age of five, children can be initiated into sewing and finger-knitting which develop fine motor control.

2. What is the best way to include chores in the child's rhythm?

   Ans: Chores are mostly an outbreath so they need to happen before or after an inbreath activity. Vigorous chores like scrubbing, sweeping, or mopping are best placed after an intense inbreath like screen use or in the afternoon when the child returns home from school. Kitchen-related chores serve as ideal transitions before and after meals (an inbreath). Taking out the next day's clothes and putting them on a hanger is a gentle chore that can happen between dinner and bedtime.

   As you become more consistent in including chores every day, a weekly rhythm can be introduced. While most chores, like setting the table before dinner, are needed every day, some chores that take more time can happen on a weekly basis. For instance, Mondays can be for baking, Tuesdays for cooking, Wednesdays for gardening, Thursdays for cleaning, Fridays for sewing and so on. This weekly rhythm ensures that the child benefits from a variety of chores, involving different types of gross and fine motor movements. Further, you can make this a learning moment by calling the days 'baking day', 'gardening day' and so on which helps the child develop the concept of time because Monday, Tuesday and so forth are abstract words with which they have no physical relationship.

Chapter 10

Sleep: The Deepest Outbreath

If you've seen a baby, you've probably noticed that they seem to doze off every now and then: while nursing, in a stroller, in someone's arms, in the middle of a diaper change. That's how naturally infants drift into sleep. Sleep feels more like home to them than being awake. The physical world is new. Being awake is exhausting. So, they drift back into sleep, again and again. Sleep is a return to the spiritual world—a world the young child is closer to than adults.

In sleep, the human being connects to the world of spirit, assimilating the day's experiences into the deepest levels of their being. Sleep is the fullest outbreath. The advice 'Sleep on it' has hidden in it the suggestion that we allow our unconscious self to find the answer or develop an idea—something the waking self can only go so far with. By stepping away from thinking actively, we invite our non-physical, non-thinking self to take hold. Often, insights to thorny problems come to us after a good night's sleep, seemingly out of the blue. Sleep is our magical friend.

Children Need to Learn the Rhythm of Sleeping and Waking

Just like it is crucial for a child to balance inbreaths and outbreaths during the day, an essential part of early childhood education is developing a healthy rhythm of sleeping and waking. As children grow, they spend more and more time being awake. The longer they are awake, the more impressions they absorb, and the more help they need to return to the world of sleep. They are learning to sleep more at night and stay awake for longer periods during the day. Because the physical world is still new to them, children need help going back and forth between the two. They need adults to help them adapt to the circadian rhythm, our earthly rhythm of light and dark.

Our World Keeps Children Awake

For a young child, going through the day is an intense sensory experience. Remember the two-hour lectures in college and the amount of information they packed in. If you zoned out, it was your body's way of protecting against a sensory overload. For a young child, every waking moment is like that—a barrage of fresh impressions. Things that adults are used to and don't even notice, for example, the honking of a passing car, can feel explosive to a child, just like a tree can withstand a storm but a strong wind can ruffle a sapling. Add to it the ringing of doorbells, buzzing of cell phones, screens flashing images wherever you go, and we have set up the child for being wide awake.

Sleep Has Fallen Off Our Radars

Meanwhile, our culture has relegated sleep to the bottom of the priority list. As we pack more into our day, sleep is pushed into a corner. Unlike junk food that upsets the stomach and demands us to take notice, inadequate sleep is easily ignored by pushing ourselves just a little more. The silent nature of sleep makes this easier to happen. There isn't a single person among us who hasn't suffered from some disturbance in their sleep life. The International Classification of Diseases (ICD-10-CM), that doctors use for diagnosing patients worldwide, specifies nine major disorders and forty-five sub-disorders of sleep, and one in three Americans suffer from them. In our drive to sustain our personal and professional lives in this fast-moving, rapidly changing world, sleep has quietly and steadily slipped off our radars.

Children Are Struggling to Sleep

If adults are reeling from a systemic deficit of sleep, young children are not far behind. At a time when they need to be learning how to sleep, they are having to navigate sleep deficits. Unlike adults, they have not yet developed the capacity to step away from the endless stream of impressions coming their way.

Sleep is the home that a young child ventures out from and yearns to return to. But the farther they travel during the day, the longer and harder it is to return at night. How often does it happen that you take your child to bed, and they start playing and running about instead of winding down? Or you start putting your child to bed, and two hours later, you're still at it and your child is wide awake? Or worse still, you tell your child it's time for bed and they start throwing a tantrum and before you know it, they're having a full-blown meltdown? What is going on here? While the clock says it is bedtime, the child is unable to wind down and fall asleep. They simply haven't had a chance to exhale all their impressions. It is no surprise then that in 2014, the American Academy of Family Physicians reported that up to half of all children experience a sleep problem.[1]

Poor Sleep Compromises Health and Learning

One of the most telling signs of poor sleep in a child is that they do not wake up in the morning on their own. They need to be woken up and often resist it. Instead of springing out of bed, they drag themselves out of it and through the rest of the day. They find it difficult to be upright. Slouching over the table, sprawled on the couch or floor,

---

[1] K.A. Carter, N.E. Hathaway and C.F. Lettieri, 'Common Sleep Disorders in Children', *American Family Physician*, Vol. 89, no. 5 (2014): 368–77, 24695508.https://www.aafp.org/pubs/afp/issues/2014/0301/p368.html (accessed 17 February 2025).

a child who hasn't slept well experiences the day as a burden. They have poor appetite and less energy to play. They may not be interested in participating in activities and you may hear about it from their teacher. Such a child may quarrel with other children over small nothings and be uncharacteristically cranky. All of these are symptoms of undigested impressions from the previous day that pull the child under as they try to begin a new day. As children grow older, poor sleep interferes with academic learning due to attention and behaviour problems. In later life, it puts them at increased risk for serious health issues, like obesity, cancer, heart disease, type 2 diabetes, high blood pressure, and dementia.[2]

What Can Parents Do to Help?

Parents create the first culture for the child. For a young child, whose development in the early years is primarily through the physical body and senses, this culture is rhythm. Because sleep is the biggest outbreath of the day,

---

[2] 'The Effects of Sleep Deprivation', Johns Hopkins Medicine, https://www.hopkinsmedicine.org/health/wellness-and-prevention/the-effects-of-sleep-deprivation

by ensuring that the child gets a good night's sleep, parents take a decisive step to create a healthy childhood.

1. Minimize intense inbreaths

Bring consciousness to all the intense inbreaths your child is getting during the day. Start by eliminating the easiest. Perhaps that is social engagements. Make it a practice to find care for your child at home if you need to go to an event that's unavoidable. Then tackle screen time, by inserting regular time for play and home chores every day. It is not enough to take screens out of your child's life; you also need to model the same by eliminating your own recreational screen use when your child is around. Keep your phone on silent or low volume. Only allow calls and messages from key people when you're with your child. Review your child's school day and how much inbreath they are getting. If it's a lot, and your child comes back drained, try to find a school that has a higher outbreath to inbreath ratio, even if it doesn't promise high academic skills. If that is not an option, make time to give your child an outbreath right after they return home.

2. Include naps and rest time

The key to falling asleep easily and soundly through the night is not to get overtired during the day. For children, daytime naps can be a big support in this regard. Often as children reach three or four years of age, they start showing less signs of tiredness in the afternoon. Usually, when this happens, parents and caregivers are quick to ditch the afternoon nap. This is a disproportionately strong response because the child ends up staying up all the way till bedtime. If bedtime gets delayed by even half an hour, the child gets a second wind and spins out. A middle path is to shorten nap time or replace it with rest time. Lying down quietly for some time in the afternoon gives the child a crucial island of outbreath that sustains them well through the evening.

3. Create a bedtime ritual

Going to sleep is a process and needs a transition. Can you as a grown-up fall asleep soon after a hectic day complete with professional and personal responsibilities? To expect a child to go immediately from busy activity to sleep is unrealistic. Your child will resist it, and you will get frustrated. What's needed is a bedtime ritual that helps the child ease into sleep. Before you get to the actual ritual, it is important to look at what the child has been doing prior to their bedtime. An overstimulated child will find it difficult to sleep. So, make sure that the child has not had continuous inbreaths in the two hours prior to bedtime, and if they have, lead them into an outbreath activity before dinner to help them exhale.

Here are five steps to consider as you create your own bedtime ritual:

- Place an anchor after dinner that signals to the child that bedtime is approaching. This could be helping the child take out their nightclothes and lay them on the bed.
- Keep time for a bath. This is relaxing and calming, especially a warm bath in winter. After they are dressed, dim the lights in their bedroom and light a candle. Let your child help you. Ask them to pass you the matchbox, for instance. The warm glow of the candle in a dark room is a centring experience for the child, away from all the daytime impressions they've had.
- When your child is in bed, give them a dry massage from toe to head. This is a relaxing experience as your touch brings their consciousness from the outside towards their own body. Tell them a simple story as you massage them. By telling the

story, you give your child a little bit of yourself as the story travels from you to them (as opposed to from a book with words and illustrations, which creates distance). Listening to a story, as they lie close to you, helps them travel into the realm of the story and away from the world around them.
- Say a verse once the story is finished. Depending on your family's values, it could be a prayer or an inspirational quote. It gently tells the child that it is time to sleep. You will find that over time your child will begin to speak it with you almost as if they are helping you help them sleep.
- Close the ritual with a simple melody sung by you, as your child gently slips into the world of sleep.

This five-step ritual may take time to put into practice if most of these are new additions to your rhythm. If you cannot do all, start with three: the anchor point, massage and lullaby. What's most important is that whatever you start with, do it every evening. Then add other steps over time. Soon you will start to see your child easing into this rhythm and having a good night's sleep.

4. Consistency

Follow the bedtime ritual every day in the same manner. Because the ritual involves the child doing things, they will start to internalize it. There will be no need to tell them or remind them. They will know what's coming next simply because they have been doing it every day.

In the beginning, keep the ritual simple by including a few steps, so it is realistic to maintain it. Once those steps are established, add more to create a full ritual over time.

Consistency might also require modifying your work commitments when necessary and sacrificing social time, all in order to protect the bedtime ritual. While it will be hard in the beginning, it will be well worth the effort when you start noticing how much health and well-being a consistent sleep rhythm brings to your child. Once the child settles into an early bedtime, you will have your evenings back.

Frequently Asked Questions

1. How do I know if my child is going to bed too late?

    Ans: Young children up to the age of seven should be asleep by 7–7.30 pm. Any time later than this and your child will find it difficult to go to sleep. The quality of their sleep will also be affected. This is because you have missed the window! There's an important window of time after dinner when a child is ready for sleep. If it is missed, you will find your child slowing down, having droopy eyes, rubbing their eyes and yawning, and becoming horizontal: rolling on the floor, curling up on the couch and wanting to be carried. Taking your child to bed when these cues start to appear is already late.

Soon after, they will get a 'second wind', which is a burst of sugar in the bloodstream. They will be energetic again and start running around, chatting and bringing toys to play with you. It will take some time until they have used up all this new energy and are able to sleep again.

2. Is my child getting enough sleep?

    Ans: First, let us look at the amount of sleep your child needs at different ages. Infants need twelve to sixteen hours, toddlers need eleven to fourteen hours, and three- to six-year-olds need ten to thirteen hours of sleep. These durations include naptimes and can vary slightly depending on your child.

Second, look for signs that tell you if your child has slept enough and the sleep has been of good quality.

- The most important sign is that the child will not need to be woken up. They will wake up on their own.
- They will actively participate in the activities at day care or kindergarten.
- And finally, they will have a good appetite and eat well at mealtimes.

3. Is afternoon nap required and till what age?

   Ans: Babies need multiple naps and toddlers can easily nap twice a day. Children three to seven years old still need to rest in the afternoon. This can be a nap or quiet time in bed. Playing with toys, reading a book or screen time do not count as rest. Lying in bed and cuddling do!

4. My child is overactive and does not want to go to bed. How can I avoid the struggle at bedtime?

   Ans: Your child may be overstimulated as they go through the motions of a day. Look at your child's rhythm and write down the details of how they spend their day. If your child's day includes the following activities, start by avoiding these disruptive experiences, especially between lunch and bedtime:

- Being on the screen

  A child who has been on the screen before their bedtime will still be processing this overload and will find it hard to go to sleep.

- Visit to a mall/play zone/arcade/birthday party/wedding

  Every time you see a child being cranky, throwing a tantrum or having a meltdown and being stubborn at a mall, a play zone or at parties and weddings, know that the child is crying for help. Through these external behaviours they are expressing their discomfort with the sensory overload that is inherent in these spaces. While malls and play zones are best avoided at all times for a young child, this is especially so when it's close to bedtime.

- Excessive physical activity

  Young children need to be in movement in a free and unstructured way. Running around, rough and tumble play outdoors is healthy for a young

child to become more aware of their own bodies and develop physical capacities. However, when it's close to bedtime, excessive physical activity for an extended time should be avoided so that it does not tire the child too much or they will have little energy left to do things they need to do before bedtime, like bathing and eating. So, observe the child for signs of petering out and that's your cue to take them home from the playground.

- Electronic music

  While music is wonderful, for young children it's best that they listen to live music and avoid electronic music. At this time, their senses are still developing and need things close to nature to be the stimulants for this growth to happen in a healthy manner. When you sing to your child, or play an instrument, even if you're not a singer or musician, the melody carries a part of you and the voice and notes are alive. Music received through electronic media is not meant for the developing sense organs. When you protect your child from overstimulation, taking them to bed becomes easier and your child will be able to transition smoothly into sound sleep.

5. Should you take your child to bed when they are falling asleep at dinner?

    Ans: Sometimes our schedules are pushed around and dinner is delayed. If you see that your child is tired and sleepy at dinner, give them a simple meal that can be eaten quickly: banana milkshake or porridge, and take them to bed.

    It is better to put them to bed when they're sleepy than delay bedtime for a full meal, bath or anything else you consider important in their bedtime ritual. This will ensure that your child gets a good night's sleep instead of having to pull through with low energy all evening.

    So next time your child looks sleepy well before their bedtime, drop everything, give them a quick meal and put them to bed. If this happens again and again, it might be time to look at their daytime rhythm.

6. Why is telling a bedtime story far better than reading with your child at bedtime?

Ans: Did you know that reading a book to your child at bedtime can interfere with your child's sleep? Bedtime stories are a wonderful part of the ritual and help parents bond with their children. But when the stories are brought through a book, simply looking at a book wakes the child up rather than help transition them to sleep! The pictures in the book and the writing have a stimulating effect on the child. And that's the last thing you want in your bedtime ritual! A healthy bedtime ritual should help a child wind down rather than wake up. So, should you take away bedtime stories? No. But there are better ways to do it that will help your child relax and ease into sleep.

- The best way is to tell a story rather than read it.
- If this is hard to do after a long day, then it is better to read from a book with no pictures. The main thing is that your child is not looking at the book but only listening to the story.

Recommended Reading

Dancy, Rahima Baldwin. *You Are Your Child's First Teacher: What Parents Can Do With and for Their Children from Birth to Age Six.* Stroud, Gloucestershire: Hawthorn Press, 2006.

Payne, Kim John with Ross, Lisa M. *Simplicity Parenting: Using the Extraordinary Power of Less to Raise Calmer, Happier, and More Secure Kids.* New York: Ballantine Books, 2010.

Steiner, Rudolf. *Practical Advice to Teachers: Fourteen Lectures, Foundations of Waldorf Education.* Great Barrington, MA, 2000.

Konig, Karl. *The First Three Years of the Child: Walking, Speaking, Thinking.* Floris Books, 2004.

Patterson, Barbara J. *Beyond the Rainbow Bridge: Nurturing Our Children from Birth to Seven.* Michaelmas Press 1999.

Glöckler, Michaela, Goebel, Wolfgang, and Michael, Karin. *A Waldorf Guide to Children's Health: Illnesses, Symptoms, Treatments and Therapies.* Floris Books. 2019.

Scan QR code to access the
Penguin Random House India website